MANAGING IT

AS AN INVESTMENT

PARTNERING FOR SUCCESS

ISBN 0-13-009627-X

90000

9 780130 096272

HARRIS KERN'S ENTERPRISE COMPUTING INSTITUTE

▼ Managing IT as an Investment: Partnering for Success
Ken Moskowitz, Harris Kern

▼ Building Professional Services: The Sirens' Song
Thomas E. Lah, Steve O'Connor, Mitchel Peterson

▼ IT Systems Management
Rich Schiesser

▼ Technology Strategies
Cooper Smith

▼ IT Problem Management
Gary Walker

▼ Data Warehousing: Architecture and Implementation
Mark Humphries, Michael W. Hawkins, Michelle C. Dy

▼ Software Development: Building Reliable Systems
Marc Hamilton

▼ IT Automation: The Quest for Lights Out
Howie Lyke with Debra Cottone

▼ IT Organization: Building a Worldclass Infrastructure
Harris Kern, Stuart D. Galup, Guy Nemiro

▼ High Availability: Design, Techniques, and Processes
Michael Hawkins, Floyd Piedad

▼ IT Services: Costs, Metrics, Benchmarking, and Marketing
Anthony F. Tardugno, Thomas R. DiPasquale, Robert E. Matthews

HARRIS KERN'S ENTERPRISE COMPUTING INSTITUTE

MANAGING IT
AS AN INVESTMENT

PARTNERING FOR SUCCESS

Ken Moskowitz

Harris Kern

Prentice Hall PTR
Upper Saddle River, NJ   07458
www.phptr.com

A CIP record for this book can be obtained from the Library of Congress

Editorial/Production Supervision: Wil Mara
Composition: Meg VanArsdale
Acquisitions Editor: Greg Doench
Editorial Assistant: Brandt Kenna
Marketing Manager: Debby van Dijk
Manufacturing Manager: Alexis Heydt-Long
Art Director: Gail Cocker-Bogusz
Cover Design Director: Jerry Votta
Cover Designer: Talar Boorujy

 © 2003 Pearson Education, Inc.
Publishing as Prentice Hall PTR
Upper Saddle River, NJ 07458

The publisher offers discounts on this book when ordered in bulk quantities. For more information contact: Corporate Sales Department, Prentice Hall PTR, One Lake Street, Upper Saddle River, NJ 07458. Phone: 800-382-3419; FAX: 201-236-7141; E-mail: corpsales@prenhall.com.

● Quoted text on page 3 is from Michael E. Porter's "Strategy and the Internet," in *Harvard Business Review*, March 2001, Boston MA. It is reprinted by permission of the Harvard Business School Press. Copyright " 2001 by the Harvard Business School Publishing Corporation, all rights reserved.
● Quoted text on pages 31 and 50 is reprinted courtesy of CIO/Darwin. © 2002 CXO Media, Inc. All rights reserved.
● Quoted text on page 40 is from Peter Drucker's "The Guru's Guru," in *Business 2.0* magazine. © 2001 Time Inc. All rights reserved.
● Quoted text on pages 40 and 42 is from Susan Ellingwood's "On a Mission," in *Gallup Management Journal*, Winter, 2001. *GMJ* info can be found on the Web at www.gallupjournal.com.
● Quoted text on pages 43-44 taken from *Boehringer Ingelheim GmbH*, Germany. © 2001. All rights reserved.

Printed in the United States of America

10 9 8 7 6 5 4 3 2 1

ISBN 0-13-009627-X

Pearson Education LTD.
Pearson Education Australia PTY, Limited
Pearson Education Singapore, Pte. Ltd
Pearson Education North Asia Ltd
Pearson Education Canada, Ltd.
Pearson Educación de Mexico, S.A. de C.V.
Pearson Education—Japan
Pearson Education Malaysia, Pte. Ltd
Pearson Education, Upper Saddle River, New Jersey

More praise for Managing IT as an Investment...

"IT managers who can bridge the strategic aims of the corporation with the nuts-and-bolts of executing an IT strategy are rare. Moskowitz and Kern go even further. They show what it takes to create competitive advantage through two key skills—how to link the entire internal and external value chains of the corporation, and how to do it in partnership with the rest of the organization. The first is a technical skill, the second, a leadership skill. Both are necessary to optimize a corporation's IT investment. This is a must-have book for all IT professionals."

Jay Bourgeois
Professor of Business Strategy,
Darden Business School
at the University of Virginia

"A clear, concise, pragmatic path to IT success. I have seen it in action—it works! This is a mandatory addition to CEO, COO, and CIO bookshelves."

Alvi Abuaf
Vice President and Director,
Global Securities Industry Consulting
for CGE&Y

"It really is critical for every individual in an IT organization to master the skills needed to partner with the business. The key to getting support and approval for IT projects is doing a better job communicating the strategic role technology plays in any company. This is the first book that describes in detail what IT managers need to do to make their organization a strategic asset that contributes directly to the bottom line."

Mark Egan
CIO,
Symantec

"Mastering the skills needed to partner an IT organization with the business is, indeed, critical. Successfully communicating the strategic role of technology is the key to obtaining support and approval for IT projects. This is the first book that describes in detail what IT managers need to do to make their organization a strategic asset that contributes directly to the bottom line."

Brian Shield
CIO,
The Weather Channel

Contents

Foreword   xvii

Preface   xix

Acknowledgments   xxi

Introduction   xxiii

Chapter 1

The Maturing of IT as a Business Discipline   1

▸ The Value Chain and the Evolution of
Information Technology   1

▸ The Message: Manage IT as a Strategic Asset   4

    Partnering for Success   4

    The Importance of Relationships   4

▸ Investing in Values   6

Chapter 2

Consequence-Based Thinking 9

▶ Big-Picture Thinking 16

▶ Tapping In 10

▶ Common Language 20

      On the Mark: The Learning Experience Company 23

Chapter 3

Partnering 25

▶ The Global Matrix-ed Organization 25

▶ Business Cases 26

▶ Business Teams 27

▶ Operating Principles 28

▶ Partnering within IT 28

Chapter 4

Value Management 31

▶ Other Examples of Communication Value 34

      Example 1: Analyst Workstation 34

      Example 2: Workflow Manager 36

Chapter 5

Strategy 39

▶ Business Strategy Formation Process 41

▶ Enterprise Vision 42

▶ Technology Vision   44

▶ Strategy   45

     Does the Firm Have Adequate Objectives?   45

▶ Making Strategy Operational   46

▶ The Importance of the Performance
Management Process   46

▶ How to Measure Progress
(Part of Marketing IT)   47

Chapter 6

The Small Picture   49

▶ Communicating the Small Picture   49

▶ How to Translate "Geek Speak"   50

▶ Meeting Management   52

Chapter 7

Organization   55

▶ Alignment with the Business   55

▶ Technology Alignment   56

     Personal Productivity Services Group   57

     Applications Architecture Group   57

▶ The Evolution of Alignment   59

▶ Personal Productivity Services Group   57

▶ Desktop Development Group   62

▶ Training Department Evolution   68

Chapter 8

Human Capital Management

75

▶ Quality of Life 77

▶ Recruiting/Hiring 77

▶ Transitioning into the Enterprise 90

▶ Mentoring for Success 90

▶ Managing the Process 90

▶ Performance Management Process 91

▶ The Organization as a Career 92

Chapter 9

Investing in Values

95

▶ How We Succeed 96

Values 96

▶ Actions as Result of Values 91

▶ The Hidden Harvest 95

▶ Values of the Saturn Car Company 96

Values 97

Mission Statement 97

Results 97

Chapter 10

CEO Roles and Responsibilities

99

▶ Leadership 99

▶	Partnership	100
▶	Education	100
▶	Flying Solo	102
▶	The Leadership, Partnership, Education Model	102

Appendix A

Sample Business Case Template

	Sample Business Case Template	103
▶	Document Overview	103
	Document Amendment History	104
▶	Project Summary	104
	Strategic Rationale	104
	Overview	104
	Action Steps	105
▶	Financial Summary	105
▶	Supporting Information	105
	Project Team	105
▶	Preliminary Requirements	106
	Preliminary Project Scope	106
	Preliminary Time/Cost Estimates	106
▶	Other Considerations	107
▶	Assumptions	107
▶	Risks	108
▶	Sign-Off	109

Appendix B

Personal Productivity Services Organization Overview

Personal Productivity Services Organization Overview — 117

▶ Desktop Development Group Overview — 117

Mission — 117

Charter — 117

Benefits — 118

▶ Training Department Overview — 118

Mission — 118

Charter — 118

Benefits — 119

▶ Help Desk — 122

Mission — 122

Charter — 122

▶ Sample Help Desk Customer Service Survey — 123

▶ Technical Support — 128

Mission — 128

Charter — 128

▶ Second-Level Support — 129

Mission — 129

Charter — 129

Benefits — 129

▶ Applications Architecture Overview — 130

Mission		130
Charter		130
Forms of Engagement		130
Roles of Architecture Group		131
▶ **Architecture Group Involvement**		132

Appendix C

Desktop Development Standards and Procedures 133

▶ **Project Lifecycle**		133
Request Management		133
Gather High-Level Requirements		134
Notifications		134
▶ **Requirements Gathering and Analysis**		135
Role Definition/Notification		136
Gathering Application Requirements		136
Cost/Benefit Analysis/Feasibility Study		137
▶ **Project Acceptance**		138
Project Charter		138
Approval/Communication		138
▶ **Project Planning**		139
List Phases, Activities, and Tasks		140
Identify Resources		140
Publish the Plan		140

▶ **Design**   140

    Reminder   141

    Documenting the Design   142

    Data Flow Diagram   142

    Entity Relationship Diagram   142

    Structure Chart   143

    Naming Conventions   144

    Relational Database: What's the Big Deal?   144

▶ **Prototyping**   145

    Technical Feasibility Prototype   145

    User Interface and Transaction Flow Prototype 145

▶ **Scope Freeze**   145

▶ **Testing (End-User Acceptance)**   146

    Test Plans and Cases   146

    Executing the Test Plan   150

    Rework   150

    Acceptance   150

    Pilot Test   150

    IT Pilot   150

    Parallel Test   151

    Training   151

    Course and Documentation Development   151

    Timing   151

Resources 151

System Administration Tasks 152

▶ **Support** 152

▶ **Marketing** 152

▶ **Implementation** 152

Technical Standards 152

Rollout Plan 153

▶ **Maintenance/Change Control** 153

▶ **Postimplementation Follow-Up** 153

System Performance 153

Process Performance 156

Appendix D

Systems Development Contract 157

▶ **User Responsibilities** 157

Project Ownership 157

Dedicated Resources 157

Sign-Off 158

System Change Control 158

Prioritization of Deliverables 158

Time Management 158

▶ **IT Responsibilities** 158

Project Ownership 158

Estimates 158

Project Documentation   159

Project Delays   159

Application Prototypes   159

System Testing   159

Time Management   159

Index   161

Foreword

In the summer of 1998, I was invited to speak at a CIO (Chief Information Officer) event sponsored by McGraw-Hill in Princeton, New Jersey. The topic for that night's discussion was: How to Build a "World-Class" Information Technology (IT) Organization. My focus was on organization, people, and process issues. One of the CIOs in attendance was Ken Moskowitz, the CIO of Standard and Poor's (S&P). S&P is headquartered in the heart of New York City's (NYC's) financial district and it is one of the many companies of the McGraw-Hill family.

Participation from the audience made the session interesting. Ken was the biggest contributor, and within minutes, I could tell that he was very much a people/process type of individual. When I finished my talk, I went over to formally introduce myself. Ken and I hit it off immediately; he had a personality that was genuine. During our discussion, he took the time to invite me to NYC to perform an infrastructure assessment of his IT department.

It was about six weeks later when I walked into S&P headquarters to do an infrastructure assessment. I started the interview process with Ken. My objective was to understand the department's issues, initiatives, and organizational structure. I started out by asking Ken how long he'd been the CIO at S&P. His answer was seven years, which surprised me.

The scuttlebutt in the IT industry is that CIOs only last about 2.5 years at any one company. The reasons vary:

- Inability to get high visibility projects done on schedule
- Company acquisition—the parent company already has a CIO
- Inability to work effectively with the business

Additionally, the CIO position is probably one of the most visible and vulnerable positions in the company.

As we continued our discussion, it quickly became apparent why his tenure had lasted so long. Ken is a sincere individual who believes and mentors his staff in values.

At the end of my first day of interviews, I felt something I'd never felt in any other IT shop. I was very relaxed—no, take that back—I was extremely relaxed. At first I didn't know what to make of it. Usually when I first arrive at a company to perform an assessment, I can feel the politics and hidden agendas in the air, but at S&P, everyone worked extremely hard, but going to work was as satisfying as being on vacation in the Bahamas. People actually looked forward to Monday morning. How could this be—how could a company with the reputation, industry name brand, and size of S&P have such a satisfying atmosphere? It was mind-boggling. Why this shop? Why S&P? Who would ever expect this type of atmosphere in NYC—certainly not I.

The two-day, high-level diagnostic focused on the organization, people, and process issues within the IT organization. The interviews involved mid-level management, senior executives, and key technical staff.

I won't get too carried away because I discovered that S&P had infrastructure issues just like any other shop. But the difference between this shop and other IT organizations was the leadership, values, and vision. By the end of Day 2, I realized that Ken's values, vision, and his demeanor flowed down the ranks throughout every part of the organization. Despite the issues (many were already being addressed), I felt that they had the potential to succeed because of the leadership. Rarely do you see a corporate IT executive respected throughout the company, but I found him at S&P.

Harris Kern
Executive Editor
Harris Kern's Enterprise
Computing Institute

Preface

This book seeks to demonstrate how the consistent application of a few very basic premises will lead to professional success (and personal satisfaction) in Information Technology.

CEO's will find what their Information Technology function can contribute and how to maximize its value to the enterprise.

Executive managers will learn how to market and enhance their value to the enterprise,

Line managers will learn how to accelerate their career path, and

Aspiring managers will understand and master the "rules of the game."

Through actual examples we will provide rules-of-thumb and an intuitive, as well as an intellectual, understanding of these basic principles.

Acknowledgments

To Mitch Fairrais and Blair Steinbach from On the Mark, Inc., for providing us with the content in Chapter 2. Their contributions played a major role with this project.

To Carol Copeland for her help in everything we needed to do to write this book.

To Doug Taggart and Steve Levy for their support, expert advice, and contributions.

To Nikki Gomez for his support, keen understanding, and insights into Personal Productivity Services. He's played a major role in making the Personal Productivity Services function what it is today.

To Stephanie Jason for her contributions and for managing one of the most efficient Help Desk we've ever seen.

To Tina Gertsch and West Nelson for taking time from their personal schedule to help us with editing.

To Leonard Kim for his friendship, wisdom, and support. Leonard (as CIO of GE Capital) has transitioned his IT organization to the level of a valuable and respected business partner.

To Richard Bentz for providing us with his insight and wisdom.

To Jack Schwartz for his valuable contributions. Jack is a good friend and is one of those rare individuals who truly understand enterprise solutions.

To Mike Graves and Steve O'Connor for letting us tap into their brilliant minds.

To Gary Walker for his contributions.

To Mayra Muniz for her support and editing contributions.

To Yogi Malcolm and Gillian Alexander for their support.

Introduction

▶ Will the Real "World-Class" IT Organization Please Stand Up?

Webster's describes Shangri-La as an imaginary, idyllic utopia or hidden paradise. For any IT professional, that usually means getting on an airplane and traveling to a resort with white sandy beaches and a beautiful ocean to de-stress. The daily pressures of IT are excruciating, and if allowed, IT professionals would hop on a plane to Shangri-La at least once a month.

Our definition of the ideal IT environment is one that is designed to exceed the enterprise's strategic goals while nurturing the individual to achieve exceptional productivity and job satisfaction. This environment can be recognized by the following signs:

- Educated and committed enterprise executive management
- Complete alignment with business goals and objectives
- Strategic decisions that accommodate a rapidly changing, dynamic business environment
- Cost–effective results
- Common architecture (i.e., processes, tools, standards, etc.)

- Individuals blossoming instead of being buried in a bureaucracy
- A culture where honesty, mutual respect, and job satisfaction flourish

In this environment, it is not an overstatement to say, "Everyone looks forward to Mondays."

The most important ingredients are executive management commitment and personal involvement. Without these, very little is possible. Even something as mundane, though of exceptional importance, as a common architecture is unachievable without genuine executive management support. The following is an example of a Standard Enterprise Infrastructure:

- Global Standard Desktop Operating System
- Global Standard Desktop Application Suite
- Global Standard Server Operating System
- Global Standard Messaging and Collaboration Platform
- Global Standard Remote Access
- Global Standard Product Platform
- Global Standard Data Backup
- Global Standard Virus Scanning
- Global Standard Server Hardware
- Global Standard Data Backup
- Global Standard Monitoring
- Global Standard Development Database
- Global Standard Development Methods and Tools
- Global Standard Desktop Hardware
- Global Standard Network

This formalized infrastructure cannot be lip service, as we have seen at hundreds of firms. True commitment means enforced decisions. True commitment requires educated understanding. It is the job of the CIO to demonstrate the relationship between understanding the strategic technology initiatives and realizing the long-term success of the firm. If executive management fails to see the value of their involvement, it is the CIO's role to change that perception or to think about his or her next career move.

▶ Why Do We Find this Environment at S&P?

We find this environment at S&P because S&P has a strong culture based on clearly understood, shared values. These shared values are not simply conceptual; they are enumerated, discussed, reinforced, and acted on. Values are guiding principles, basic beliefs that are fundamental assumptions on which all subsequent actions are based. As a whole, values define the personality and character of an individual or group. Values are the essence of an individual or group and provide guidelines by which to make consistent decisions. In reality, values are ideals that are indicative of one's vision of how the world should work.

▶ The Value and Purpose of this Book

This book seeks to demonstrate how the consistent application of a few very basic premises will lead to professional success (and personal satisfaction) in IT.

- Chief executive officers (CEOs) will find what their IT function can contribute and how to maximize its value to the enterprise.
- Executive managers will learn how to market and enhance their value to the enterprise.
- Line managers will learn how to accelerate their career paths.
- Aspiring managers will understand and master the "rules of the game."

Through actual examples, we will provide rules of thumb and an intuitive, as well as intellectual, understanding of these basic principles.

THE MATURING OF IT AS A BUSINESS DISCIPLINE

META Group research shows that 70% of IT organizations are still perceived as cost centers by their business counterparts, rather than as value centers.

▶ The Value Chain and the Evolution of Information Technology

"The basic tool for understanding the influence of Information Technology on companies is the value chain—the set of activities through which a product or service is created and delivered to customers (see Figure 1–1). When a company competes in any industry, it performs a number of discrete but interconnected value-creating activities, such as operating a sales force, fabricating a component, or delivering products, and these activities have points of connection with the activities of suppliers, channels, and customers. The value chain is a framework for identifying all these activities and analyzing how they affect both the company's costs and the value delivered to buyers...

1

Inbound Logistics	Operations	Outbound Logistics	Marketing and Sales	After-Sales Service
Real-time integrated shipping, warehouse demand management and planning, and advanced planning, and scheduling across the company and its suppliers	Integrated information exchange, scheduling, and decision making in in-house plants, contract assemblers, and components suppliers	Real-time transaction of orders, whether initiated by a customer, salesperson, or channel partner	Online sales channels, including Web sites and marketplaces	Online support of customer service representatives through e-mail response management, billing integration, co-browse, chat, "call me now," voiceover-IP, and other video streaming
Dissemination throughout the company of real-time inbound and in-progress inventory data	Real-time available-to-promise and capable-to-promise information available to the sales force and channels	Automated customer-specific agreements and contract terms	Real-time inside and outside access to customer information, production logs, dynamic pricing, inventory availability, online submission of x quotes, and order entry	Customer self-service via Web sites and intelligent service request processing, including updates to billing and shipping profiles
		Customer and channel access to product development and delivery status	Online product configurators	Real-time field service access to customer account review, schematic review, parts availability and ordering, work order update, and service parts management
		Collaborative integration with customer forecasting systems	Customer-tailored	
		Integrated channel management, including information exchange, warranty claims, and contract management (versioning, process control)	Push advertising	
			Tailored online access	
			Real-time customer feedback through the Web	

Figure 1–1   The Value Chain

"The evolution of Information Technology in business can be thought of in terms of five overlapping stages, each of which evolved out of constraints presented by the previous generation. The earliest IT systems automated discrete transactions such as Order Entry and Accounting. The next stage involved the fuller automation and functional enhancement of individual activities such as human resource management, sales force automation, and product design. The third stage, which is being accelerated by the Internet, involves cross-activity integration, such as linking sales activities with Order Processing. Multiple activities are being linked together through such tools as Customer Relationship Management (CRM), Supply Chain Management (SCM), and Enterprise Resource Planning (ERP) systems. The fourth stage, which is just beginning, enables the integration of the value chain and entire value system, that is, the set of value chains in an entire industry, encompassing those of tiers of suppliers, channels, and customers. SCM and CRM are starting to merge, as end-to-end applications involving customers, channels, and suppliers link orders to, for example, manufacturing, procurement, and service delivery. Soon to be integrated is product development, which has been largely separate. Complex product models will be exchanged among parties, and Internet procurement will move from standard commodities to engineered items.

"In the upcoming fifth stage, Information Technology will be used not only to connect the various activities and players in the value system but also to optimize its workings in real time. Choices will be made based on information from multiple activities and corporate entities. Production decisions, for example, will automatically factor in the capacity available at multiple facilities and the inventory available at multiple suppliers. While early fifth-stage applications will involve relatively simple optimization of sourcing, production, logistical, and servicing transactions, the deeper levels of optimization will involve the product design itself. For example, product design will be optimized and customized based on input from factories and suppliers but also from customers."[1]

[1]Porter, Michael E., "Strategy and the Internet," *Harvard Business Review*, March 2001.

▶ The Message: Manage IT as a Strategic Asset

The increasing complexity of each stage of the value chain along with the continuing evolution of technology have resulted in a fundamental integration of technology within and across every stage of the value chain. IT has become mission-critical and needs to be managed as a strategic asset. It is inseparable from the business and requires complete alignment with business goals. Successful IT executives need to consider themselves and convince others to consider them as part of the business, not separate from the business.

Partnering for Success

IT needs to be organized to rapidly respond to the needs of individual business groups. This requires a planning process tightly integrated with each business group and an enterprise-wide vision within which all of these needs can be met. This can only be accomplished by establishing working relationships at individual and group levels with all business partners.

Business teams, including IT as a "business," must work together. Other than enterprise infrastructure, there is no such thing as an IT project. Whether IT is responsible for 10% of the tasks or 90% of the tasks, IT is merely a member of a business team, led by a business project champion. All projects require business unit champions and business project champions.

All members of this business team must be scheduled with accountabilities and deliverables. Priorities must be determined through jointly developed business cases. All projects must build a business case—a technology case is not sufficient. All business cases should discuss the alignment of objectives with enterprise objectives (see Appendix A for a sample business case template).

The Importance of Relationships

Good relationships are critical for good partnerships. Relationships need to be continually nurtured. Relationships also need to become institutionalized; they must be grown beyond individual relationships to departmental relationships. These relationships must be viewed by the enterprise as value-added. A partner's perspective and needs must be anticipated. In other words, a good partner answers a question before it is asked.

Relationships, while strongly encouraged on an individual level, need to be understood on a group level. For example, if a particularly difficult partner has been unable to form a relationship with the technology staff, the technology department must recognize this and take steps to forge the right relationship. Senior technology managers should identify the sources of the relationship problem and proactively correct them. This may involve issues of competence, mutual respect, credibility, business knowledge and perspective, communication, etc. Relationships are not built overnight and require patience and consistency. Every communication is a relationship-building opportunity.

IT needs to review its relationships on a regular basis as part of standard management process. IT partnering/relationships depend strongly on senior management support. The tone is set at the executive or senior management committee level. Relationships are built from the top down and bottom up, but may not rise beyond a certain level in the organization without active senior management support. Sometimes a whispered word in the right ear works wonders (a requirement of true senior management commitment).

Delegate relationships upwards, downwards, and sideways. Avoid jealously guarded relationships; they defeat the purpose.

A purchaser/contractor relationship is transitory and dependent on circumstances at a certain point in time. A partnering relationship encourages shared goals and objectives. Partners understand the need to accommodate because their relationship will exist beyond the current assignment. Partners do favors for each other and prevent one another from making mistakes.

IT is no longer a cost center and a growing number of highly successful firms are recognizing this. IT is an investment and should be managed as such to increase revenue and profits. However, recognizing and managing IT as an investment rather than a cost center is a difficult task and requires a significant cultural shift in most companies.

Figure 1-2 Investing In Actions

▶ Investing in Values

The environment, as we have described it, is illustrated in Figure 1-2.

This picture is incomplete. Something is missing. The actions we need to take must be consistent, strategic, adaptable, and repeatable under dynamically changing circumstances. The missing piece is values. The complete picture is shown in Figure 1–3.

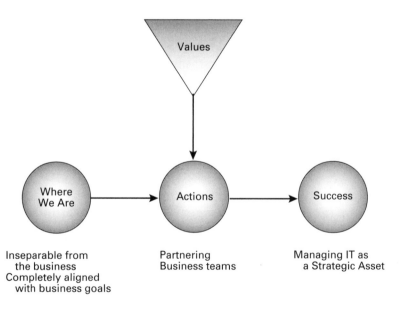

Figure 1-3 Investing in Values

Values are guiding principles, basic beliefs that are fundamental assumptions on which all subsequent actions are based. As a whole, values define the personality and character of an individual or group. Values are the essence of an individual or group and provide guidelines by which to make consistent decisions (for a complete description and discussion of values and their role within an organization, please refer to Chapter 9, "Investing in Values").

CONSEQUENCE-BASED THINKING

Consequence-based thinking means making decisions that are influenced and driven by desired consequences rather than limited by the situations you face. The hallmarks of an environment where consequence-based thinking exists are:

- People no longer fear sharing ideas because they aren't worried they will be scrutinized as individuals based on how right or wrong their ideas are. They operate with the security that others will recognize that every idea put forward increases the odds of achieving the desired consequence. Every idea becomes either the next useful idea or leads to the next useful idea. Either way, every idea is valued and seen as useful.

- People become very focused on the desired consequence. The energy in the organization becomes channeled to that end.

- People begin to value the power of questions instead of believing that all the power resides in the right answer. More great questions get asked and ultimately lead to better processes and efficiencies that serve the enterprise.

- Ideas are generated as the catalyst for subsequent ideas and the pressure of finding absolute solutions or final answers dissipates, enabling more and often better thoughts to flow with ease.

9

- The hero mentality goes away. The thinking that "If I get the one idea that gets the right result, I will be the hero and honored by my company or colleagues" becomes obsolete. It is replaced by a sense that everyone plays a role in contributing to an outcome. Great outcomes feel like shared victories.

- People don't feel the pressure to individually go for 100% solutions. They can work toward the beginning of a solution, confident that the team will help hone the process to create the desired solutions.

- The culture becomes one of accepting mistakes with the recognition that it is necessary to make mistakes to achieve success. There is much more "grace" and "dignity" available for human beings in such an environment. (With every attempt to create a working light bulb, Edison did not see failures, but rather recognized he was getting closer to his desired end.)

- When people become consequence-minded, they become open to new processes to get to the desired consequence versus becoming attached to the existing situation or current way of doings things. They say, "How do we create this result?" versus "What's the best we can do given the situation we face?" As they become less attached to their current situation or way of doing things, out-of-the-box thinking and solutions begin to become the norm.

- The environment supports making decisions that are influenced and driven by desired consequences rather than limited by situations.

Typically, the decisions people make and actions they take are driven by responding to situations. The situation defines and limits their view of the possibilities and they end up doing "what's possible" based on the situation.

Consequence-based thinking, however, insists that the desired consequences be the main driver of the decisions or actions *independent* of the current situation. Decisions or actions are sought that produce the desired outcome as opposed to decisions that are justified by and viewed as "making the best of a situation." As a result, consequence-based thinking creates solutions that are not limited by the situation. Creativity becomes necessary (and often apparent), resulting in the transformation of a situation into something completely new and different.

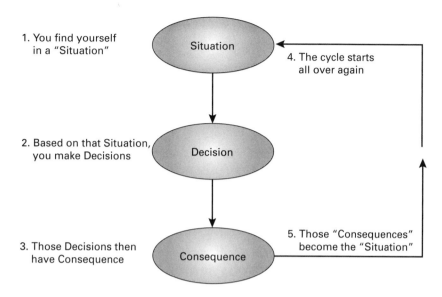

1. You find yourself in a "Situation"

Situation

4. The cycle starts all over again

2. Based on that Situation, you make Decisions

Decision

3. Those Decisions then have Consequence

Consequence

5. Those "Consequences" become the "Situation"

Figure 2–1 Situation, decision, and consequence model

Consequence-based thinking comes from our situation, decision, and consequence model depicted in Figure 2–1.

Essentially, we propose that when people are faced with situations, they make decisions. Those decisions have consequences. The consequences then become the new situations.

For example, imagine a situation where your partner phones and asks you to pick up some milk on your way home from an evening out. It's late. You feel tired. Your fatigue allows you to justify the decision not to stop to pick up milk. The next morning, you wake up for your morning ritual of a big bowl of Mega Puff cereal, only to find yourself in the situation of having no milk for your breakfast feast. Your decision not to stop for milk had a consequence. That consequence then became your new situation.

People in any situation typically base their decisions on one of two things: the situation they face or the consequences they desire.

Most people base the vast majority of their decisions on the situation they face at any given moment. It is far less often that human beings choose to make decisions aligned with creating the consequences they desire. We believe those who are more consistently able to make

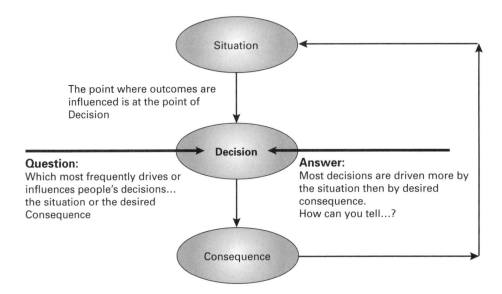

Figure 2–2 On The Mark's Situation–Decision–Consequence model

decisions based on "desired consequences" get more of what they want out of life and work.

We call the ability to make decisions based on desired consequences "consequence-based thinking" (or, from Figure 2–2, "below-the-line thinking"). We call making decisions based on a situation "situation-based thinking" (or, from Figure 2–2, "above-the-line thinking").

Sometimes we will refer to people and their decisions as being "consequence-minded" or "situation-minded," depending on where in our model their focus was when they made decisions.

How do you know when you are "above the line" (or focused on the situation) when you make a decision? One of the indicators is that you find yourself *justifying* your action or decision based on the situation. You might find yourself saying, "I did that because..." and then offer a description of the situation, designed to justify your response to it.

Another indicator is your need to show that what you did was "right." We call this the "right/wrong trap," where you forfeit the desired consequences for the privilege of being "right." We never have to defend our actions if the consequences are superb; but when the consequences are less than what we had hoped for or don't justify our actions, we

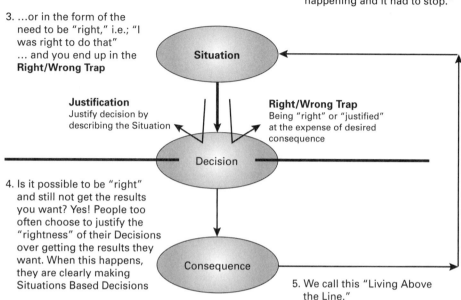

1. ...people ask why they did what they did. Most often you will get a description of... *the situation!*

2. This usually takes the form of Justification for a Decision that is rooted in the Situation, i.e.; "But he did this" or "this was happening and it had to stop."

3. ...or in the form of the need to be "right," i.e.; "I was right to do that" ... and you end up in the **Right/Wrong Trap**

Situation

Justification
Justify decision by describing the Situation

Right/Wrong Trap
Being "right" or "justified" at the expense of desired consequence

Decision

4. Is it possible to be "right" and still not get the results you want? Yes! People too often choose to justify the "rightness" of their Decisions over getting the results they want. When this happens, they are clearly making Situations Based Decisions

Consequence

5. We call this "Living Above the Line."

Figure 2–3   Living above the line

fall into the right/wrong trap and feel the need to show how "right" our decisions were given the situation.

How can you tell when a decision was driven by the situation (see Figure 2–3)?

Conversely, when you make a decision from a consequence-based mindset (think below the line), you tend to feel no need to defend your decision because you recognize it as moving you toward the desired consequence (see Figure 2–4).

When applying the model (see Figure 2–5) to groups of people who work together, there is less concern about who has the *right* answers or who made the *right* decisions if the focus becomes making decisions that bring the group closer to the desired consequences. Workgroups that become consequence-minded don't care or focus on whose decisions are right and whose are wrong because they recognize that sometimes the next idea or decision is necessary to lead to the next and

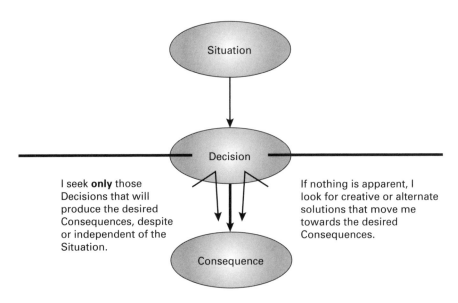

Figure 2–4 Living below the line

the next, until ultimately the desired consequences are achieved. Each idea is not measured by whether it is right or wrong. Each idea is used as a catalyst or springboard to the next idea. As a result, every idea is valued.

With the application of consequence-based thinking, people recognize that ideas build on ideas and that one person's work builds on another's. People recognize that it is not any one person's responsibility or efforts alone that lead to the answers that will get to the desired consequences. Therefore, the focus on any decision is not whether it is right or wrong, but rather what can be learned from it that will propel the group to the next step in achieving the desired consequences.

Individuals are organized into workgroups, which need to be aligned to ultimately serve the true purpose of the existence of the organization—the "enterprise."

It is important that individuals in any part of a business understand how they connect to and serve the overall enterprise of the business. This is particularly relevant for those in IT positions.

This alignment begins with an understanding of the enterprise. Sadly, many get so caught up in the portion of the work of the business they do, they either do not have the opportunity to understand the nature

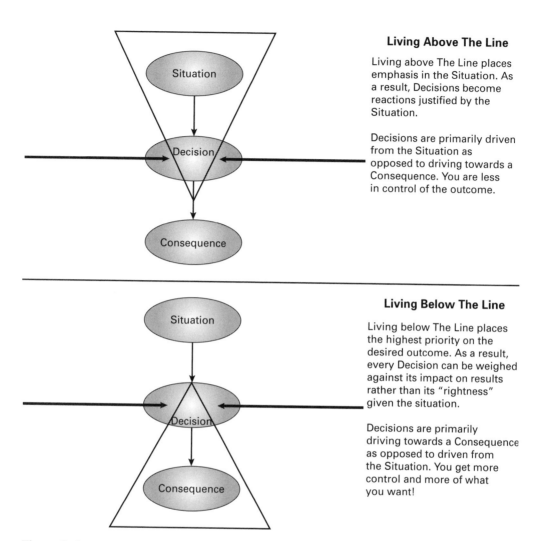

Living Above The Line

Living above The Line places emphasis in the Situation. As a result, Decisions become reactions justified by the Situation.

Decisions are primarily driven from the Situation as opposed to driving towards a Consequence. You are less in control of the outcome.

Living Below The Line

Living below The Line places the highest priority on the desired outcome. As a result, every Decision can be weighed against its impact on results rather than its "rightness" given the situation.

Decisions are primarily driving towards a Consequence as opposed to driven from the Situation. You get more control and more of what you want!

Figure 2–5 Living above and below the line

of the true enterprise, or they lose sight of it in the heat of everyday endeavors. A commitment to serve the enterprise is different than a commitment to serve a workgroup or team.

It is equally important, however, for individuals to understand how they connect to and serve their own workgroups, department, and the organization as a whole, and how that "system" supports the enterprise. It is also important for individuals to understand how they connect to and serve other workgroups and departments to work synergistically within the organization for the success of the enterprise.

Individuals should measure their decisions and actions in light of how they will serve the enterprise of the business, not merely by how well they will serve the outcome of a project or the needs of a department.

It is key that members of IT teams see themselves and their work as core to the business itself and not view the IT function as an appendage of the business. IT is an integral thread that is woven throughout all aspects of the business. The rest of the organization is unlikely to see it as such if the IT team does not see itself this way and does not approach each endeavor with this mindset.

As members of IT teams understand their place in the organization and that they serve the enterprise and not merely other departments in the organization that serve the enterprise, it is likely that others will view them as critical and necessary partners that can be trusted to provide solutions that don't merely serve a process, but truly serve business outcomes. As a result, they will gain more opportunity to influence their internal clients with appropriate solutions. This view of their role, combined with their understanding and commitment to the enterprise, will allow them to create solutions that go well beyond the needs expressed by internal clients to ultimately benefit the overall business.

▶ Big-Picture Thinking

As other areas within the organization recognize IT's ability to understand and connect its endeavors to the true enterprise, the more likely other areas within the organization will be compelled to view IT as a business partner and trusted advisor rather than a service organization or resource.

The technology organization needs to understand the desired consequence, "la raison d'être" of the enterprise, and where it is required to be as an organization. Each technologist must understand where he or she is in the enterprise, and how he or she and his or her workgroup serves the enterprise. Everyone needs to see the big picture.

- Big-picture thinking is key to becoming consequence-minded. The greater the opportunity to see the big picture, the more likely people will be able to step into consequence-mindedness.
- Big-picture thinking creates context and enables people to honor the values they seek to live (and work) by. Most people are not

typically drawn to or motivated by values. More typically, people are drawn to outcomes.

- The clearer you make the enterprise, the easier it is for people to understand and embrace the values that enable the enterprise, even if they would not necessarily choose those values in their personal life.

- The more connected and integral people feel to the enterprise, the less likely they are to subscribe to the "us versus them factor." People feel connected to the enterprise through understanding the big picture. As a result of not subscribing to the "us versus them factor," they are less likely to disregard the enterprise's values in dealing with others because they feel more akin to and related to others with whom they share the enterprise.

- When it's time to make a judgment call, people are more likely to make one in favor of the enterprise. This supports enabling decisions to be made on the battlefield in the midst of action with confidence.

- Big-picture thinking is all about clarity as to where people are headed so that everything they do is aligned with the enterprise. With the big picture clearly in mind, every decision they make and every action they take can be considered in light of how it supports or hinders the enterprise.

  Well-managed IT teams do their work in the context of the big picture. Everyone understands how the IT team is linked to the success of the enterprise as a whole and thus the success of the organization. They do not work on a project with the project itself being the largest view they have of the enterprise; rather, they view each project they engage in within the scope of the larger enterprise and where the business as a whole is headed. This enables them to act as partners in the business rather than just worker bees, since seeing their place in the success of the enterprise enables them to make decisions and put forward innovative suggestions that go beyond simply meeting the technical requirements requested by their client groups. Their ability to add value, if they have big-picture understanding and a big-picture mindset, increases dramatically.

One old story that illustrates the relationship between big-picture thinking and quality of work goes something like this:

A traveler comes across three bricklayers on a scaffold. The traveler asks the first bricklayer, "What are you doing?"

The first responds, "I am earning a wage."

The traveler then asks the second bricklayer, "What are you doing?"

The second responds, "I am building a wall."

They are doing the same "work." Which of the two is laying the brick better?

The traveler then asks the third bricklayer, "What are you doing?"

The third responds, "I am building a cathedral."

This story illustrates the power big-picture thinking has on the everyday work of "laying bricks." Said another, more personal way:

- I can't as easily find my sense of purpose without the big picture.
- Everything I do becomes more meaningful when there is context.

The more meaningful an enterprise becomes to *individuals*, the more effort people exert to bring about success. This is very different from a mission or vision statement that is "owned" by an organization and not by its individuals: When a mission/vision is owned by an organization, you get bricklayers earning wages; when a mission/vision is owned by individuals, cathedrals are built.

▶ Tapping In

Definition: Tapping in is the deliberate act of proactively stepping in to add value to any part of the organization where you see there is opportunity to give insight, add perspective, "nudge" or bring correction to a person or process, or add value by appropriate, unsolicited action.

- It is in direct opposition to observing others within the same enterprise and rolling our eyes, shaking our heads, or offering negative comments in response to them doing things inefficiently or doing things that impede or do not lead/contribute to success.

- It means always feeling enough accountability for the enterprise's success to react to ALL colleagues' efforts proactively and constructively.
- It is about helping others (and therefore the enterprise) get it right rather than making others wrong to feel good about comparative contributions.
- It means having the mindset of a PARTNER who has responsibility for the enterprise in its entirety and is therefore proactive in insuring actions (ours and others) align with moving the enterprise to success, as quickly and efficiently as possible.
- It means we are all responsible for each other and everything relates to an enterprise objective (value).
- It requires honesty and candor (value).
- Its emphasis is on relationships (value)—you need to have the right relationships to tap in. Without the right relationships, the organization will not have the benefit of tapping in as part of its culture.

People don't tap in in an above-the-line culture (reacting to the situation, not the desired consequences).

- Tapping in means putting consequences ahead of situations.
- Ironically, most people would welcome more "taps" because they feel like they are alone, trying to carry the responsibility of something greater than they are.
- People resist "taps" because taps often come in unskillful, critical ways. The more skilled a group becomes at tapping in, the more welcome taps become.
- IT needs to become skillful at "tapping in":
    - Relationships
    - Partnering
    - Productivity
- Most people agree that tapping in is a good thing, but it is not the type of behavior witnessed often in organizations. The question is why isn't it happening?
    - Fear of ruffling the next person's feathers?
    - Fear of not getting it right?
    - Fear of someone saying, "See, I told you so?"
- People don't tap in because they feel the need to be "polite," not wanting to interrupt or cause the other person to feel like they are not doing an adequate job.

- Tapping in is being a good corporate citizen (value) and being accountable for the enterprise.
- Never personalize anything (value). When living "above the line," you personalize everything. When you operate above the line (meaning you look only at the situation when you have an opportunity to tap in), you worry that the person you are tapping in on is going to take it personally. If everyone operates "below the line," meaning they are consequence-minded and operate in a culture that supports consequence-based actions, it's very hard for anyone to see tapping in as a personal affront. Instead, all parties involved should welcome tapping in as a means of moving the enterprise forward.
- Tapping in is congruous with the following philosophy: "Seek a solution—don't simply highlight the deficiencies" (value).

"Ideas building on ideas" needs to replace the concept of good and bad ideas or finding the "one right solution."

▶ Common Language

I have often said that I am unsure whether, in my lifetime, I have ever seen two people actually in the same conversation. Although I say this for emphasis, as dramatic as it may sound, I wonder how close to the truth this statement may be. Seldom do people engaged in a single conversation walk away with the same understanding of what was being discussed.

Words are nothing more than attempts to represent thoughts. These thoughts, however, are rarely outside the life context and greater understanding of the communicator. Every word carries with it the potential of a lifetime of associated meaning, experience, belief, and assumption. This seems obvious when we examine words like "love" and "honor," but what about words like "commitment," "important," and "deadline?"

As a result, seldom in any communication, whether it be in person, by phone, or in writing, do the originator of any thought and the recipient of that thought understand the intended thought in the same way. In most circumstances, including those in the context of business, people believe they are on the same page with others (colleagues, coworkers, employees, clients, other departments, etc.) when, in fact, they are very often on very different pages when it comes to their respective understanding of the same discussions or communications in which they all participated.

Many organizations experience high degrees of stress, anxiety, confusion, and overlap of work in opposition to the efforts of others (often unknowingly) because they hold a very different understanding of the same communications or discussions and simply don't realize there may be discrepancies between their understanding and the understanding of those they depend on or interact with. This phenomenon is far more prevalent in organizations than most recognize. It undermines our ability to work in synergy with others, even those within our own ranks.

One of the opportunities to minimize this phenomenon and to maximize the possibility of people walking away from every communication or interaction with common understanding is to very consciously strive to build a "common language" into the everyday banter of an organization, language that is clearly understood and carries common meaning for all parties in any communication or interaction. This language is most effective when crafted from common experience, where participants actually experience a concept with all its unexpressed subtleties and associations, and name it something that evokes a much fuller understanding of the issue or idea.

This is not always possible. As a result, in every communication (verbal or written), it would serve the originator of that communication well to step into the frame of reference of the recipient of the communication and carefully craft his or her words to create meaning from within the mindset of the target audience.

For instance, if I were speaking to a cartographer about a location on a map, I would probably use language such as "the location just to the east of X" as opposed to "the location just to the right of X," knowing the cartographer is far more likely to "think" in terms of north, south, east, and west.

Just as I would use different words to deliver a message to a group of young children than I would to deliver the same message to a group of senior managers in an organization, every effective IT manager should consider his or her audience to seek to craft the best words and "common language" that will create the strongest likelihood of understanding for the audience and therefore the strongest likelihood for successful communication. (Successful communication is communication that accomplishes what it sets out to do. It doesn't matter how "good" or "clear" or "two-way" or "well written" it is; if it doesn't accomplish what it set out to accomplish, it was not successful!)

For instance, in any interaction that involves instruction or direction, it is key to use language that will be clearly understood by the recipients of the communication (those who will use the direction or instruction). They will need a clear understanding to achieve whatever the instruction or direction is intended to guide them to accomplish, so the communication should be as tailored as possible to their understanding.

The onus is clearly on the originator of any communication to find the right language to be clearly understood by whomever they are communicating to. This pertains to any portion of a conversation you participate in as well as other types of communication.

When IT departments learn to speak the language of other business disciplines (Marketing, Sales, Finance, Human Resources, etc.), they may suddenly find an ability to create agreement in those areas and move forward with dramatic increase in their ability to bring about appropriate technical solutions to business challenges.

Likewise, as IT teams learn to speak the language of other business disciplines, respect for IT increases and others view IT more and more as a critical business partner, committed to providing world-class business solutions. They begin to include and rely on IT for insight they may not have recognized before. The ability to use common language breaks down the "us versus them" factor that often undermines IT's ability to work synergistically with other areas of the business.

When it comes to our own ranks, we need to be equally vigilant. It is here where our assumptions that "we are all on the same page" are most dangerous. We should never assume any given word or phrase means the same thing to our peers or colleagues as it does to us, even if we have used that word or phrase with each other for a long period of time. We need to check our respective definitions of the words and phrases we use with one another, often and continuously, if we have a serious desire to work with significant levels of synergy.

On The Mark: The Learning Experience Company

The content for this chapter was provided by On the Mark. On The Mark is a Toronto-based company that specializes in experiential learning. They provide extraordinary learning events that truly impact people's productivity. Their contact information is:

Mitch Fairrais
416-255-5066
www.onthemark.ca
info@onthemark.ca

3

PARTNERING

▶ The Global Matrix-ed Organization

An effective way to view the world is through a global organization matrix as illustrated in Figure 3–1. The matrix highlights the three dominant views of the global organization:

- **Local view**—The perspective of a business unit within a geographic region.
- **Regional view**—The perspective of a geographic region across multiple business units.
- **Global business unit view**—The perspective of a business unit across multiple geographic regions.

These three views respond to interdependent market demands and compete for enterprise resources. IT resources, when viewed through the matrix, can be allocated visibly and objectively if the competing business needs are presented through business cases developed jointly by IT and its business partners.

Jointly developed business cases will institutionalize IT's alignment to the business and tie IT activities to the creation of value for the enterprise.

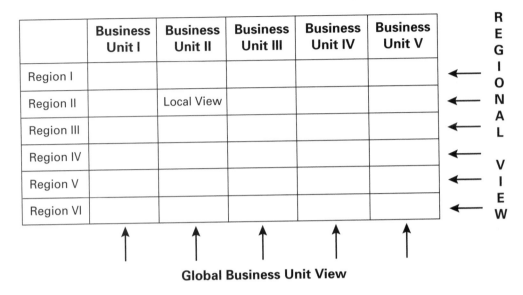

Figure 3–1   Global organization matrix

▶ Business Cases

Business cases should be required for all work outside of routine maintenance and minor enhancements. Business cases (a sample business case template can be found in Appendix A) are the instruments through which project priorities are created and set by a joint business unit/technology team. It's a business case, not a technology case. Business cases are required to address questions of enterprise business goals and technology goals. The business case process forces individuals and organizational units to engage in a continuing dialogue.

Alignment with business objectives is a natural consequence of jointly developed business cases for projects that fall within the business's strategic plan. Approval of the business case moves the business agenda forward and creates partnership and understanding during the process. A not insignificant objective of this process is the respect of the business for IT's understanding of the business and its strategic needs.

Business Teams

Business teams represent the fundamental relationship for identifying, specifying, prioritizing, and creating IT value. Business's role as a partner of IT rather than a consumer of IT is institutionalized through this relationship. As shown in Figure 3–2, every technology project is done within the context of a business team. Business and IT staff are paired, and every project has a business unit champion and a business project champion. All members of the team have accountability as well as responsibility. The business team concept is so important that the business case template explicitly requires the business unit champion and the business project champion to be named. Our goal is a consequence-minded culture: It's not about someone being right; it's about getting to the right solution. Everyone owns the problem and everyone owns the solution. Refer to Appendix D, "Systems Development Contract," for an example of accountabilities and responsibilities.

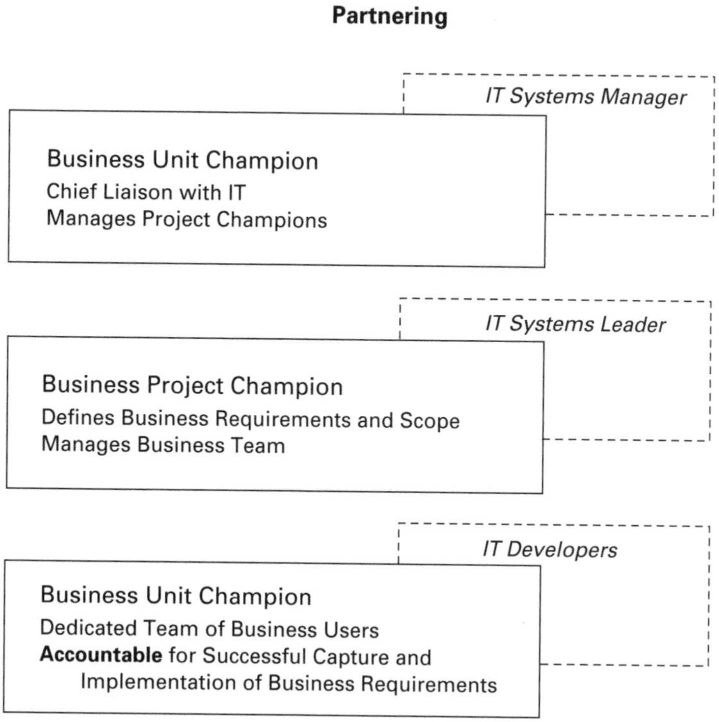

Partnering

Figure 3–2   Partnering

▶ Partnering Within IT

Every member of a department needs to understand and be kept up-to-date on any information that relates to what they are doing and what their partners are doing. Delegation of authority to the lowest practical level allows new ideas to be tested constantly on the front lines in multiple situations simultaneously. Many opportunities are recognized only at the front lines. These opportunities may be fleeting if not recognized at the source when they occur. Delegation encourages creativity. Over-communication is demanded. Managers will never have as much information as all of their people on the front lines. Relevant information must flow upwards and downwards with enough breadth to allow individual perspectives to be applied. A manager cannot be at every subordinate's shoulder at every minute of every day. Every subordinate needs to be able to react, make decisions, and inform the manager of relevant facts.

All staff members need to be mentored to recognize these opportunities. Opportunities may result in efficiencies, operational effectiveness, cost savings, new markets, competitive advantages, or strategic shortcomings. The gathering of intelligence takes place at all levels of the organization. The analysis of this intelligence likewise takes place at all levels of the organization. A free flow of intelligence needs to take place continuously. The synergistic application of human experience to this flow of intelligence leads to far more effective solutions than a simple hierarchical structure can hope to achieve. It is the exact opposite of information hoarding. Information hoarding is an obstacle to success. Information sharing is partnering.

The resolution of IT as a business partner is illustrated in Figure 3–3.

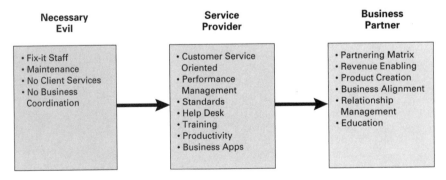

Necessary Evil
- Fix-it Staff
- Maintenance
- No Client Services
- No Business Coordination

Service Provider
- Customer Service Oriented
- Performance Management
- Standards
- Help Desk
- Training
- Productivity
- Business Apps

Business Partner
- Partnering Matrix
- Revenue Enabling
- Product Creation
- Business Alignment
- Relationship Management
- Education

Figure 3–3 Evolution of IT

▶ Operating Principles

The operating principles of managing IT as a cost center and managing IT as an investment are contracted in Table 3–1.

Table 3–1 Managing IT as a Cost Center vs. Managing IT as an Investment

Cost Center Management	Managing IT as an Investment
Business throws projects requirements over transom (often as solutions masquerading as requirements).	Business teams including IT as a "business" work together to specify requirements.
Priority set by user intuition.	Jointly developed business case used to determine priority.
Acceptance testing done by users when time permitted.	Acceptance Testing done to exacting standards and scheduled with accountabilities and deliverables.
Infrastructure as a reactive afterthought.	Strategic architecture/infrastructure as a competitive advantage.
Application development as an art.	Application development as a science (discipline and rigor).
Infrastructure as overhead.	IT Infrastructure as an Internal Service Provider.
Task-related communication (isolated).	Relationships.
Accept user requirements verbatim. Even worse, creating user requirements without the user.	Ask the right questions and jointly specify requirements.
Noniterative requirements document.	Prototypes and proof of concepts.
Projects belong to IT only.	All projects require business units champions and business project champions.
Technology for technology's sake.	Alignment with business objectives.
Reactionary/task-oriented.	Proactive/relationship-objectives.
Working in silos.	Teamwork/synergy.
Mistrust.	Credibility.
IT for IT's sake.	Customer-centric.
Lack of metrics.	Performance metrics.
Bureaucratic.	Adaptable.
Follow orders.	Creative solutions.
Authoritarian decision making.	Decentralization of decision making.
Cost containment.	Build for efficiency and effectiveness, architect for growth and business alignment.
Vendors managed by the users.	Vendors managed by IT.
Vendor invoices go to the user.	Vendor invoices go to IT.

VALUE MANAGEMENT

As we said earlier, successful IT executives need to consider themselves and convince others to consider them as part of the business, not separate from the business. "In organizations where IT is viewed as extremely critical to the business, today's CIO has not only realized that marketing the IT organization furthers the awareness that IT adds value to the business, but also has acted on that realization through concerted efforts to market IT...more than 70% of Global 2000 organizations perceived their IT units as supporting the business: They have a cost center, 'just-keep-the-lights-on,' service-utility mentality that maintains IT should be mostly transparent to the rest of the business. If things are going well, no one knows the IT organization is there. If things are going badly, it gets noticed...leading CIOs are focused on bringing the full value of information to the enterprise's bottom line...because business exists more and more at the discretion of information, IT organizations need to sell to their business colleagues the fact that IT can and should be leveraged for business value and growth. Marketing the IT organization increases the correct perception that IT adds value to the business...marketing the IT organization raises the enterprise's recognition of its dependence on the IT organization and helps ensure the CIO is (and is perceived to be) a business partner."[1]

[1] *The CIO Desk Reference*, Metagroup 2001.

A 1998 Pricewaterhouse-Cooper study of the 436 fastest growing U.S. companies found 60% of CEOs agreed IT was either critical or extremely critical to the business. Firms in which the CEO rated IT as "extremely critical" to the business showed 72% greater annual growth than firms whose CEOs rated IT as "critical" to the business. During a 10-year period, these same firms achieved a 45% better compound annual growth rate than firms whose CEO rated IT as "neutral."

The marketing of IT is a conscious attempt to identify, contribute, and clearly communicate value. Whether value is measured through revenue enhancement, operational efficiency, or competitive advantage, it needs to be communicated in nontechnical terms. Wherever possible, value should be quantifiable and measurable. Keep the business aware not only of status, but also direction. Use your business champions as evangelists. Keep the executive committee in mind (anecdotes, key high-level accomplishments, letters of praise). Operational advances can be demonstrated via "day-in-the-life" scenarios.

There are also times when the forest cannot be seen for the trees. Small pockets of value may sometimes indicate a larger need. The Desktop Development Group at S&P is a good example of identifying a forest from the trees.

Recognizing value is often a bottom-up process. Such was the case in recognizing the concept of an application spectrum and creating S&P's Desktop Development Group to provide value to single users and small workgroups. S&P's IT Training Group was staffed with professional trainers who trained S&P business staff in the use of desktop tools. Several years ago, the members of this group began to find themselves answering questions and assisting analysts and editors with basic macro creation. They began official training courses in macro writing, which allowed them to leverage end-user skills and knowledge to the benefit of the organization. But they also began to recognize that departmental priorities rarely reflected single user or small group productivity needs and that exposure to IT was generally only through the help desk or large applications. The application spectrum (see Figure 4–1) allowed them to recognize that there were categories of applications from repetitive keystroke macros all the way up to industrial-strength three-tier applications.

At the left end of the spectrum, we find single user and small group productivity projects that can be completed in three hours to three

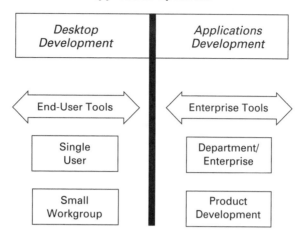

Application Spectrum

Desktop Development	Applications Development

End-User Tools

Enterprise Tools

Single User	Department/ Enterprise

Small Workgroup	Product Development

Figure 4–1 Application spectrum

weeks. At the right end of the spectrum, we find large departmental and enterprisewide projects taking 3–12 months to complete. The tools and perspective at points along the application spectrum are different and are designed to service different audiences. For example, the left side of the spectrum uses tools like VBA and Access to bring simple but effective productivity improvements straight to the desktop in a personal way.

This application spectrum exposed many users to IT's value powerfully and directly because of the speed of implementation and the very real and immediate quality-of-life improvement. They suspected that a very quick response to a small group's needs repeated for many small groups was an opportunity to add value to the enterprise and at the same time establish relationships all across the organization. To quantify the value of this opportunity, they transferred one of their trainers into a one-person group for 12 months. They carefully assigned desktop projects and quantified the resulting benefits. At the end of the 12 months, their results were better than they anticipated. They determined that for every hour of desktop development, they achieved an 80-hour annual savings in analyst support time. This allowed them to create a small Desktop Development Group and institutionalize the process.

▶ Other Examples of Communicating Value

Value should be quantifiable and measurable. It is best to communicate a value in its simplest recognizable form. For example:

Unedited Version	Value Communication Version
We built a robust, flexible editorial platform that is scalable and automates the editorial process utilizing redirectional metadata technology to deliver abstract, encapsulated information.	We built a reliable and flexible editorial tool that gathers, presents, and delivers customized information to our clients. The tool reduces product creation time by 40% and can deliver information in any industry standard format without requiring technical intervention.

Value is best communicated to the enterprise by IT's business partners. The right relationship and recognition of value lead to the ideal situation of business partners becoming evangelists. At a fundamental level, it needs to be understood (without having to say so) that underpinning the entire process of value creation is the partnering relationship. All members of IT need to be educated to recognize their business contributions. All need to understand their business partners' concerns and address them both formally and informally.

The following real-life examples illustrate value communication in different circumstances:

Example 1: Analyst Workstation

Background:	Multiple desktop tools
	No reliable network
	Obsolete hardware and software
	General perception of value to be obtained, but no visceral appreciation of potential value; therefore, no incentive to make the necessary investment to move forward
Objective:	Create a desktop environment and infrastructure that allows analysts to do their jobs more effectively.

Issue:	How to demonstrate the value of the proposed desktop (and its supporting infrastructure)
What was done:	Selected an influential managing director (MD) who recognized the value of the desktop.
	The MD became a partner and was instrumental in the development of the workstation prototype. The MD also encouraged other analysts to work with the team.
	Made the workstation an analyst creation that IT would implement.
	This was not an IT creation or project.
	Helped the MD to document actual examples of daily workflow and proceeded to automate that workflow with real data within the prototype. This was not a production prototype, so work was illustrated through screens only.
How value was communicated:	Performed "A Day in the Life of 'Rob Analyst'" for executive audience. Rob and two analysts from his team were the starring actors.
	Three PCs were set up at tables in a large conference room. All three PCs were connected to the network and had their monitors displayed on a large screen at the front of the room.
	Act I took an actual workflow with actual data and illustrated how data was gathered, manipulated, analyzed, shared, and put into a product. This included all the manual handoffs and redundant effort with hours required illustrated.
	Act II ran through the proposed workflow with the same cast, using the same information and the new workflow.
	Reinforcement was made through activity reports and presentations (e.g., postimplementation reviews).
Results:	The play resulted in a standing ovation. The audience not only recognized the value in a personal way, but also added significantly more potential value with

immediate suggestions for present and future enhancements.

Not only did this exercise communicate value, but communicated vision as well.

When this initiative came up for funding, it had already become a road show and was warmly approved.

Example 2: Workflow Manager

Background:	Inconsistent processes across workgroups.
	Current processes required centralized groups.
	High volume could only be handled by expanding staffing.
	Enterprise expansion called for decentralized groups in geographically dispersed offices.
	Expenses were growing too rapidly to meet increased volume.
	Desire to avoid hiring "to peak" and being overstaffed at some future date.
	No availability of management information.
Objective:	To enable geographic decentralization, improve the processes of the analytical groups, and capture the management information necessary for the administration and control of the new unit.
Issue:	How to measure value beyond simply "allowing the physical moves to happen."
What was done:	A dedicated project team staffed with analysts and technologists re-engineered the workflow, automated the new processes, trained everyone to obtain maximum value from the new approach, and set up help desk specialists to ease the transition.

How value was communicated:	Measurements were easily captured and clearly understood by all.
	System was designed to capture measurement information.
	Baseline (before) data was collected for comparison with new (after) measurement data.
	Measurements included average time for completion (by category of deliverable), deliverables/office, and deliverables (by category)/analyst.
Result:	Business unit proudly presented the results to the executive committee, which became an evangelist.

STRATEGY

Strategy requires a big picture and a roadmap to get there. Remember the big-picture analogy used in Chapter 2?

- Everything becomes more meaningful when there is context.
- The more meaningful an enterprise becomes to individuals, the more effort people exert to bring about success. This is very different from a mission or vision statement that is "owned" by an organization and not by its individuals. When a mission/vision is owned by an organization, you get bricklayers earning wages; when a mission/vision is owned by individuals, cathedrals are built.

Just as every brick is laid with an understanding of its role in the cathedral, every project undertaken by technologists needs to be related to its role within both the enterprise vision and the IT vision. This leads to a counterintuitive truism: All operations are strategic and all strategy is operational.

Strategic thinking is not a once a year process or a road to a document; it is a perspective that can be developed and taught. It is a behavior that can be learned and must be reinforced at all levels of the organization. "The ability to connect one's job to a larger mission is not primarily a matter of competence, work ethic or other such traits that good workers naturally possess. Instead, the job-mission connection comes about through communication that starts at the executive level and resonates throughout the ranks."[1]

Strategic thinking stresses an enterprise point of view over seat-of-the-pants, silo thinking. An interesting example is acquisition planning and its attendant, due-diligence. Enterprise acquisition strategy may require the integration of technology, emphasize economies-of-scale, and require product integration, marketing integration, supply chain integration, etc. It may even require consolidation, complete independence of businesses, or any variation in between. IT needs to be part of every due-diligence effort and needs to budget and plan accordingly. While it is unlikely that technology will become a deal-breaker, it can happen. Appropriate due-diligence that incorporates integration planning avoids the untenable situation of building "islands of automation" through short-term thinking. The result is an expensive and noncompetitive enterprise with little ability to react to its marketplace.

"*The Practice Of Management* in 1954 was the first book to ask the question: 'What is a business?' No one had ever asked that question before. They thought we knew, and I asked that question because my clients asked it. I was a securities analyst 70 years ago in London, so I can say that no financial man will ever understand business because financial people think a company makes money. A company makes shoes, and no financial man understands that. They think money is real. Shoes are real. Money is an end result. What is a business? The only function of a business is to create customer {value} and to innovate."[2] The "financial man" is a powerful example used by Drucker, but is by no means the only example of such thinking. In the technology arena, we often encounter technologists who implement technology for technology's sake.

We are all in the business of contributing to the creation of customer value and innovation. Thinking strategically means making consistent decisions that incorporate foresight. Conversely, trendy decisions are often inconsistent and rarely synergistic. Thinking strategically means understanding and planning for the implications of decisions. It means being proactive, not reactive. We can proactively make a decision that is counter to our technology strategy for a clear business purpose, but it must be done consciously and with a plan to converge eventually

---

[1] Ellingwood, Susan, "On A Mission," *Gallup Management Journal*, Winter 2001, p. 7.

[2] Drucker, Peter, Business 2.0, *The Guru's Guru*.

Business Strategy Formation

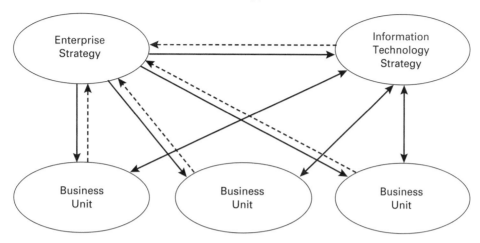

Figure 5–1 Business strategy formation process

with the enterprise technology strategy. It means that we do not avoid the tough questions to simplify a short-term decision. For example, it is not enough to put together a disaster recovery plan for technology without pressing the organization to confront the issue of business continuity. Business continuity is often reduced to disaster recovery and left in the hands of IT. If this is the case, it is incumbent on the CIO to educate executive management on the need for a business continuity plan and the role of technology within such a plan.

The business strategy formation process sets the context that relates an enterprise to individuals and individuals to an enterprise. A simplified illustration of the business strategy formation process is shown in Figure 5–1.

▶ Business Strategy Formation Process

Enterprise strategy is the cornerstone of the business strategy formation process. Enterprise strategy forms business unit and IT strategy, which in turn influence enterprise strategy. However, business unit strategy and enterprise IT strategy are more interdependent and are created in partnership. This is an arduous and exacting process that begins with a vision.

Companies whose employees understand the mission and goals enjoy 29% greater return than other firms.[3] Vision statements need to obey some fundamental principles; they should be:

- Simple
- Clear
- Timeless
- Powerful
- Memorable
- Actionable

What many executives don't realize, however, is that a company's mission statement can also be a management tool. But, it is only useful to the extent that each employee links the mission to his or her job. "High scores on the... mission question correlate positively to all desirable business outcomes... but especially to productivity and profitability. This is validated quite effectively in Figure 5–2. The ability to connect one's job to a larger mission is not primarily a matter of competence, work ethic, or other such traits that good workers naturally possess. Instead, the job-mission connection comes about through communication that starts at the executive level and resonates throughout the ranks. The best statements... are short, direct, and set a value system."[4]

▶ Enterprise Vision

Boehringer Ingelheim GmbH, Germany, with seven billion dollars in revenue, is one of the world's 20 leading pharmaceutical companies. It has a particularly well-written vision statement that can be summarized in three words: Value Through Innovation. This is simple, clear, timeless, powerful, and memorable, and, by itself, insufficient. By itself, it is a slogan. When explained within a vision, it becomes actionable.

---

[3] Watson Wyatt Work study

[4] Ellingwood, Susan, "On A Mission," *Gallup Management Journal*, Winter 2001, p. 6.

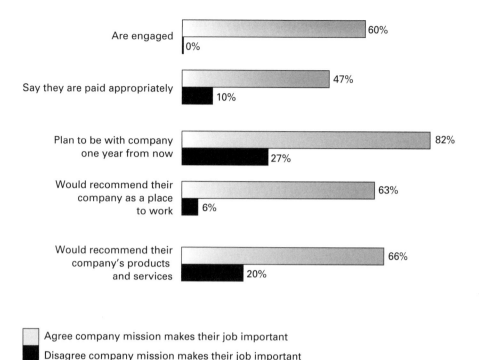

Figure 5–2 Esprit de Corps

- *Boehringer Ingelheim's* corporate vision is founded on five key principles, statements which together form a shared ambition and worldwide commitment:[5]
- Change is our opportunity—Without change, there can be no progress.
- Value will be our competitive advantage—In a competitive world, we expect our customers constantly to demand more for less.
- Innovation in everything will be our challenge—We will only deliver outstanding value to our customers if we are innovative in everything we do.
- Waste is our enemy—We need to have one of the lowest cost bases in the industry if we are to deliver outstanding value to our customers.

---

[5] © 2001 *Boehringer Ingelheim GmbH*, Germany. All rights reserved.

- Our distinctive character is our strength—We are world-wide and measure ourselves against world-class standards. Yet we are also a corporation with family traditions in which people are valued as individuals.

Collectively, these principles add up to Value Through Innovation, the vision that strengthens *Boehringer Ingelheim*'s business worldwide and keeps it more competitive.

An enterprise vision is a prerequisite to a successful IT vision, and an enterprise strategy is a prerequisite to a successful IT strategy. It is the CIO's responsibility to educate the CEO on the need for both an enterprise vision and an enterprise strategy.

▶ Technology Vision

Vision statements can take many forms. A rather unique form of technology vision statement can be found at Hershey Foods, Inc.

Hershey Foods Corporation and its subsidiaries are engaged in the manufacture, distribution, and sale of consumer food products. The company produces and distributes a broad line of chocolate and non-chocolate confectionery and grocery products. Hershey is currently the U.S. market leader in chocolate confectionery. Hershey's vision is to continually create value for shareholders, customers, and consumers as a focused, branded, global chocolate and confectionery snack company.

Hershey's technology vision is stated in a rather unique form. The format is powerful and memorable:

- *D* isciplined
- *I* nvestment guided by
- *S* trategic architecture that supports
- *C* ollaboration across the organization through
- *I* ntegration of
- *P* rocesses and people that facilitates
- *L* earning,
- *I* nnovation, and
- K*N* owledge to yield
- *E* nterprise results

▶ Strategy

Technology strategy creation must be implemented as a continuous business process. It is an analytical, operational, and creative process that does not result in a volume collecting dust on a shelf. The resulting strategy and the continuing process of strategy evolution need to be communicated in the "common language" that we have spoken about. This is not to say that the technology strategy does not need to be written at a detailed technical level—still trying to avoid impenetrable jargon—but there needs to be higher level sections that speak directly to our business partners derived through a collaborative process. The value and contribution of technology to the future success of each business unit and the enterprise should be clear.

The characteristics of a successful technology strategy and process are:

- Clarity
- Executive management participation
- Business unit collaboration
- Linkage with business unit processes
- Continuous evolution rather than annual re-creation

Does the Firm Have Adequate Objectives?

The META Group states: "Traditional IT strategic planning is a yearly, typically static and discrete process. It takes considerable time (often four to six months) to produce a large, static document that details projects and timetables from a technology versus business viewpoint. Our research shows strategic IT planning is evolving away from this traditional approach toward a dynamic and continuous process... Leading Global 2000 organizations (< 20%) will adopt this dynamic process as an IT planning best practice by 2003/2004. They will achieve both a significant competitive edge and improved IT employee morale as a result, having achieved continuous, ongoing alignment of IT initiatives with business imperatives and opportunities. By 2004/2005, most Global 2000 organizations (> 75%) will adopt traditional IT strategic planning as a best practice, while the leading-edge organizations (< 20%) will have fully integrated business and technology strategy planning into a seamless, ongoing value organization process."

Making Strategy Operational

As important as it is to institutionalize the strategy creation process, it is equally important to institutionalize a continuous dialogue between the strategy and operational decisions. It is reasonably straightforward to institutionalize higher level dialogues such as collaborations between the enterprise and its business units, the business units and IT, and IT and the enterprise; however, it is much more difficult to bring this down to a personal level.

If individuals and groups are making decisions in a larger context, they are making enterprise decisions. It is the manager's job to continually reinforce larger objectives from the team leader on up. A sense of context is a necessary component of team meetings. Whether the group is a full business team or only IT, it is important to remind the team of its context within a larger group objective and the enterprise objective. Never let the team forget where it fits in and what it is contributing. There are times when the context will drive the team members to alternative and far more valuable solutions. This contribution to value is impossible without context.

Two effective ways to keep strategy in front of individuals are through business cases and the performance management process. As discussed in Chapter 3, "Partnering," business cases should be required for all work outside of routine maintenance and minor enhancements. Business cases (a sample business case template can be found in Appendix A) are the instruments through which project priorities are set and created by a joint business unit/technology team. Keep in mind that they are business cases, not technology cases. Business cases are required to address questions of both enterprise business goals and technology goals. The business case process forces individuals and organizational units to engage in a continuing dialogue.

The Importance of the Performance Management Process

The performance management process needs to include agreed-upon personal goals and objectives. These goals and objectives should be part of the annual appraisal process. Not only do they need to be reviewed annually, but they also need to be revisited at least semi-annually to ensure that all individuals and all levels of management are continually challenged to address their roles in meeting enterprise goals and objectives. This process needs to be given serious attention because it is often too tempting to treat this discussion superficially. Management at every level needs to be engaged and held accountable for a productive dialogue to take place.

▶ How to Measure Progress (Part of Marketing IT)

Strategic progress needs to be demonstrably evolutionary; continuing progress should be visible over a multiyear period. Annual technology plans should be placed side by side over multiple years and progress matched to enterprise goals and objectives. Operational and tactical successes should be viewed in the overall strategic context. Annual plans should fit neatly together as stepping stones to strategic goals. This presentation should be updated annually and presented to the executive committee of the corporation. Progress and obstacles to progress should be concisely presented. This presentation is itself a very useful tool for the marketing of IT.

THE SMALL PICTURE

Once the big picture and a roadmap to get there are in place, every individual needs to understand how their tasks fit into the big picture and how this relates to them on a personal level. We call this the small picture. The small picture is closely related to that part of human nature that asks, "What's in it for me?" This is not meant to imply a selfishness or self-centeredness on the part of the individual; it merely recognizes that each of us understands best when we understand personally. In other words, the conceptual big picture and the personalized small picture form the opposing ends of a communication spectrum.

▶ Communicating the Small Picture

The small picture is a particularly powerful concept for presentations and management meetings. Communications must be clear, concise, valuable, jargon-free (see Figure 6–1), and remembered. To align with the business, we must speak the language of the business and relate "tech speak" to "What's in it for me?" Never miss an opportunity to relate a concept to a real-life benefit. This educates the consumer, demystifies jargon, and allows value to be clearly seen. A particularly powerful presentation technique is "a day in the life." An influential user or group of users of a new system should condense their day and illustrate it (playing themselves) as they tackle a real-life situation.

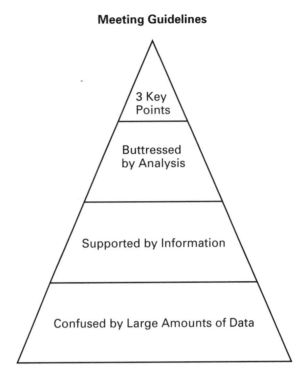

Meeting Guidelines

3 Key
Points

Buttressed
by Analysis

Supported by Information

Confused by Large Amounts of Data

Figure 6–1 Communicating the small picture

Act I should show the group under current circumstances and Act II should show the group under the new and improved circumstances. The benefits of the new and improved circumstances should be clear to all in the audience with little to no explanation necessary. The narration and explanation should come from the business partners using the system, not from IT.

▶ How to Translate "Geek Speak"[1]

You've probably said something like it 20 times a day while bantering with your IT colleagues. "Let's take this ERP discussion offline with Chuck, who can penetrate the FUD on this." This makes perfect sense

[1] Blodgett, Mindy, *CIO Magazine*, December 15, 2001.

to your network manager, but your CFO (chief financial officer) will be baffled. As you prepare to do battle with that same CFO over your budget, being clear and concise is more important than ever.

So the next time you're in the boardroom trying to sell upper management on a plan to migrate away from your company's legacy systems, don't speak geek. Instead, speak the language of business. Here's a guide to help you translate some examples of techy talk into the kind of lingo any CFO (or CEO) can understand.

"We'll need to kludge around a bit to fix that bug in the system."
Translation: "We're going to avoid some computer problems by working around them."

"This will give us a multitier architecture that's low maintenance, flexible and robust."
Translation: "The technology is useful, cheap and it won't break."

"We have very scarce PC real estate."
Translation: "We don't have room on this computer for all those nutty programs you want to add."

"Version 5.1432 of Acme Technology's new suite of integrated KM, CRM and ERP wireless tools suffers from software bloat."
Translation: "This software contains more features than we'd ever need, and it's too complicated to run."

"The vendor is gonking when he tells you the software will instantly give us a robust SFA system"
Translation: "They're lying. That sales-force automation product doesn't work."

"We've got to get rid of this meat loaf."
Translation: "We're going to install a system to block the jokes, pyramid messages, and other useless e-mail."

"I realize that this m-commerce software has a lot of object value."
Translation: "I know you really want this wireless e-commerce technology, but let's figure out what it does before we buy it."

"I can leverage that inventory-management module across multiple channels."
Translation: "I can track inventory online and in our stores."

"That consultant thinks he's a member of the digerati."
Translation: "That guy says he knows something about computers and the Web, but he's clueless."

"Promising to install an ERP system in two weeks was a real CLM."
Translation: "Now that I've deep-sixed my career, what kind of severance package do you think I can get?"

▶ Meeting Management

Senior management attention spans can be remarkably short. We need to communicate with clarity and ask ourselves what it is that we wish the audience to take away from the communication. The communication, to be successful, needs to meet an objective. The objective needs to be planned prior to the communication; for example, what three points do we want the audience to remember? Assuming that the audience does not have a photographic memory and does have a short attention span, we need to be able to anticipate their perspective. We need to identify the audience and anticipate their questions. We need to understand the audience and their concerns. We need to package the content to match the audience's level of understanding and communications style.

Meeting management is a skill that can be learned. Meetings should be planned and expectations should be managed. Meetings should be kept as short as possible. Every participant should leave every meeting understanding why the meeting was held and recognize the value of having attended the meeting. The oft-repeated dictum: "Tell them what you're going to say. Say it. Then tell them what you've said." is always appropriate. The three key points are what the audience will remember. The analysis, which buttresses these key points, will likely be remembered rather vaguely. The value of the analysis is in supporting the key points, and if successfully done, gives validity to the key points such that the key points will be remembered appropriately.

Depending on the level of the audience, the analysis may be supported by information. However, to descend into further detail distracts the audience with large amounts of data that cloud the clarity of the entire presentation. Make your points as succinctly as possible and don't explain more than the audience needs to hear. The key points need to be validated by analysis and supported by information, but it is only the key points that the audience will truly remember.

Every slide needs to be reviewed by asking the following question: "What do you want the audience to take away from this slide?" The big picture of the communication is the three points the audience will take away. The small picture of the communication is a personal appreciation of what the big picture means. At every step of the way, remove excess verbiage, filler, and anything that distracts the audience from the three key points.

Meetings are excellent mentoring tools. Meeting management is an excellent vehicle for the constant reinforcement of strategies, values, operating principles, and relationship-building principles. Technology managers should be challenged to manage their meetings to achieve success in all these areas. The planning of a meeting and a post-mortem should be viewed as learning experiences.

A practical rule of thumb is that all meetings should end with clearly identified action items.

Training courses in presentation and written communication should be required for all project managers throughout all levels of IT management. Everyone should communicate effectively. We stress over-communication; this does not mean a volume of communication that overwhelms the senses, but rather, a constant reinforcement of big-picture context and small-picture content. Reinforcement of key points fosters organizational memory and concentrates attention on the forest rather than the trees.

ORGANIZATION

Alignment with the business needs to be more than a strategic plan or a written set of operating principles. The IT organization needs to be set up in a way that allows business alignment to flow as a natural consequence of the way a job is done.

▶ Alignment with the Business

To align with a business, you need to be able to react both functionally (e.g., deep technical skills) and geographically (e.g., globally, regionally, locally) to business initiatives. The solution is a matrix organization that combines shared services with personnel dedicated to business units at the global, regional, and local levels. This can accommodate any enterprise needs by strengthening or weakening "dotted lines" and/or "standards/guidelines."

The only way to align with a business is to become part of the business. Dedicated applications development staff, physically sitting with the business, having its operational priorities set by the business, participating in business operations and strategy, and having its budget overseen by its line of business forces technology to be aligned with the business. The key to the matrix is that these groups, for all practical purposes reporting to various lines of business, report on a straight line to technology and on a very strong dotted line to the business. Therefore, these units are part of the business, but ultimately reports to technology. The management principles to be followed are a strict adherence to joint understanding and no surprises. The business priority is to discover and prioritize opportunities and needs, while the technology priority is to offer practical solutions. The systems manager in charge of such a group must represent both IT to the line of business and the business unit to IT. This position in a matrix organization requires the ability to report to multiple managers and be an honest advocate for each. Success requires the appropriate personality as well as the appropriate culture. Taking the time to find and train capable systems managers is critical. The organization may be right, but will still not function properly without the right people in these key positions. They need to understand the business, the personalities, and the technology without letting ego enter into the equation.

The systems manager is the single point of contact between the business units and IT. A many-to-many relationship is counterproductive. All activity is coordinated through the systems manager, who must avoid the trap of becoming a bottleneck. A large part of this role is as a traffic cop, participating directly only in those activities that require a systems manager's direct involvement. The systems manager has direct control of the business unit's dedicated application development staff and coordinates the business unit's use of shared technology services.

Shared services provide specialty skills that may not have critical mass within each business unit and need to be managed for the enterprise to leverage skills, obtain economies-of-scale, and maintain an application architecture. Specialty skills may include database administration, system administration, help desk, and network administration. Shared services are traditionally and almost exclusively found in infrastructure or data center groups. However, technology as a business partner has now evolved beyond this model of shared services. The Personal Productivity Services Group and Application Architecture Group are critical, new shared services organizations, neither of which report through the data center hierarchy.

▶ Technology Alignment

A successful technology organization can take many forms, but should include a Personal Productivity Services Group and an Application Architecture Group.

Personal Productivity Services Group

A Personal Productivity Services Group integrates support personnel and personal productivity applications at the desktop and individual levels. It is technology with a human face. It is composed of the help desk, first- and second-level support, training, and desktop development. The Desktop Development Group (introduced in Chapter 4, "Value Management") exposes many users to IT's value powerfully and directly because of the speed of implementation and the very real and immediate "quality of life" improvement. This very quick response to individual and small group needs repeated for many small groups is an opportunity to add value to the enterprise and at the same time establish relationships across the organization.

Help desk, first- and second-level support, training, and desktop development services are all delivered to an individual or small group rather than to a department. These are the personalized services of technology. By delivering these services through one organizational unit, support services are integrated in a very personal, visible, powerful, and synergistic way. It is a constant reminder to the business that technology is friendly and beneficial, and it is a constant reminder to IT that customer service is its central function.

Applications Architecture Group

The Applications Architecture Group is the guardian of the application platform. This standard set of tools, procedures, programming techniques, object libraries, and interfaces is the mechanism through which all global application development is created, maintained, and leveraged. For example, if one business unit's Application Development Group is developing a module that could be leveraged by the enterprise, rather than being created multiple times, an architect will modify the module into a reusable object that all development groups can utilize. This modification, which is of great value to the enterprise, is done without forcing the business unit to change its deliverable for the enterprise.

The Applications Architecture Group also provides standards, mentoring, highly competent SWAT team resources, and complex technical solutions. Additionally, this group serves as an in-house technical consultant.

These skills are not unique to a shared services group. What is unique is it's the group's position within the organization. It reports to the Global Application Development Group, not to the data center or CIO.

Historically, the architecture function came out of the data center organization. Data center resource planning was originally the only meaning of architecture. Technical services became a centralized unit for systems management, database management, and networking, while hardware planning, storage management, and capacity planning were handled by various other units within the data center. There was a lesser need for an Applications Architecture Group due to the nature of the centralized mainframe environment; the operating environment of the mainframe dictated application architecture. This application architecture consistency became lost when technology evolved to a client/server environment and integration of a bewildering number of tools and systems became a new requirement. Then, application architecture was no longer as straightforward and needed to accommodate a dynamic application environment.

In the past, the data center organization always centralized architectural decision making within the various groups that could be brought together to plan and maintain an infrastructure platform. However, when the application development organization no longer had the luxury of an application platform being a direct result of the infrastructure platform, it needed its own architects who could affect infrastructure platform decisions and build an application platform on top of the infrastructure platform.

Some firms have tried assigning overall architectural decisions to an architecture group reporting to the CIO. This has not proven effective. The tendency is for an "ivory tower" to develop and for white papers to substitute for practical decisions. Real architects need to keep their hands dirty. Architects should have responsibility for real deliverables. Recommending something that one must live with and not something for others to use focuses the mind and results in something useful. By keeping close to application front lines, architects understand subtleties that drive application developers crazy. This relationship between application architects and developers leads to a very powerful and practical application architecture.

The Evolution of Alignment

The maturing of IT as a business discipline began with IT as a necessary evil, moved on to IT as a service provider, and has progressed to IT as a business partner. Table 7–1 illustrates this evolution.

Forming an Applications Architecture Group is not a totally new concept and it's the group's position within the IT organization that needs to be considered very carefully. However, the Personal Productivity Services Group is a new concept and needs to be reviewed in greater detail. An overview of the Applications Architecture Group can be found in Appendix B.

Table 7–1 Evolution of Alignment

	Necessary Evil	Service Provider	Business Partner
INFORMATION TECHNOLOGY	Maintenance	Customer service oriented Performance management Metrics Standards	Strategic Asset Aligned with the business
APPLICATIONS DEVELOPMENT	Back office	Productivity tools Management information Back office	Revenue enabling Product creation Workflow management
PERSONAL PRODUCTIVITY SERVICES	Nonexistent	Workstation Support Training Help Desk	Desktop Development Education Integrated support Personal relationships
APPLICATION ARCHITECTURE	Dictated by mainframe O/S. No application architecture group needed	Discipline and consistency of mainframe world is unavailable as an enterprise solution Systems integration shows the need for an application architecture Application architects only available through consulting firms and systems integrators	Strategic architecture includes adaptable application architecture Aligned with the business: Operating efficiencies Leveragable Speed to market Cost-effective Web enabled

▶ Personal Productivity Services Group

The four organizations of the Personal Productivity Services Group are:

- ◆ Desktop development
- ◆ Training
- ◆ Help desk
- ◆ Technical support

The Personal Productivity Services Group introduces the concept of a Desktop Development Group and an expanded training function. These two groups, when tightly integrated with a customer service-oriented help desk and customer service-oriented Technical Support Group, produce the Personal Productivity Services Group. Figure 7–1 illustrates the tight integration.

Information management has become a critical element in business today. When information is effectively managed to maximize business opportunities, competitive advantage, and customer satisfaction, its value far outweighs the cost of the hardware and software tools that support it. However, information management systems do represent

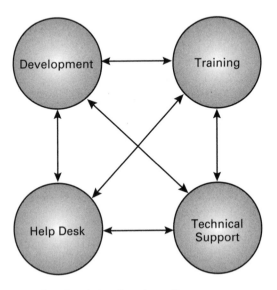

Figure 7–1 Personal Productivity Services Group

a significant investment, and it is very important to manage them effectively. That management has changed dramatically over the past several years. The plunging cost of computer equipment (in relation to exponential growth in capability) has prompted not only new tools for managing information, but whole new ways of thinking about managing information.

Computerized data at the personal and workgroup levels has become an important part of the information infrastructure. A recent industry study found that about 80% of all corporate information is stored in MS Office files—more specifically, an inventory at a Fortune 500 company found over one *million* MS Office files, roughly 860 for every staff member. Almost 75,000 Word and Excel files were found to contain macros, with 70% of them in Excel files. That volume of data and the trend it represents command some attention and raise a number of issues, such as:

- How much of that information is duplicated in other places? Are these data stores consistent? What is the cost of duplicated resources for storage and processing? Are erroneous business decisions being based on inconsistent information?
- How much of that data could be put to use by other organizations if they knew it existed?
- What business rules are embedded in those macros? Are those rules documented anywhere? Are they being consistently applied across workgroups, or for that matter, across different spreadsheets of the same user?

Parallel to the explosion in desktop data is the explosion in desktop tools; in other words, with all of that data being stored on the desktop in Word and Excel files, obviously those applications have become major tools for managing corporate data. This issue raises more questions, such as:

- How much time are people spending creating and managing information tools (e.g., macros) rather than on their primary jobs?
- Are they using the right tools for the job? For example, is data being managed in Excel when a database is more appropriate?

The Desktop Development Group and an expanded training function evolved from the recognition of these issues and the need to do something about them.

▶ Desktop Development Group

The Desktop Development Group provides:

- **Desktop development services**—Single user and small workgroup systems for most types of applications as well as administrative and operational automation on both the departmental and enterprise scales.
- **Consulting management**—Leverages end-user development and provides assistance in managing external service providers.
- **Third-level support and management**—Directly addresses the above issues and many others that are important to the managers and users of information management technology.
- **Data consistency**—Guides users in the management of information sources and storage. For example, certain kinds of data should only be drawn from corporate databases and not stored locally. The Desktop Development Group can help users set up extract processes and manage updates to ensure that the data used for decision making is current and consistent.
- **Expanded uses of data**—With a cross-organizational scope of services, the Desktop Development Group is in a unique position of awareness of existing processes and data sources that may be adapted to new uses. A company that can develop a corporate memory and leverage its experience has a strategic edge in meeting customer needs.
- **Business rule management**—Again, with its cross-organizational view, the Desktop Development Group can help to identify common business rules and processes and can help to standardize their implementation.
- **Staff utilization**—A key objective of the Desktop Development Group is to make its clients more effective in accomplishing their goals. It can do this by:

- Fully assuming the role of the desktop developer, allowing users to focus on their operations rather than building systems.
- Coaching and counseling users who do their own development, sharing the experience of the professional Desktop Development Team.
- Assisting users with project management.

- **Tool utilization**—With a broader collective base of experience in development than any user, the Desktop Development Group is in the unique position to advise on the most appropriate tool for a particular job, and to provide the hands-on expertise to make it work. For example, the Desktop Development Group can advise when a database is more appropriate than a spreadsheet, and can actually assist with the implementation of that tool. Also, the group's design, coding, and testing guidelines can help to make development more consistent within and across business units. One of the many advantages of this is that consistent screen design and navigation within applications can allow managers more flexibility in staffing tasks, since an employee's basic knowledge of one application will be transferable to another.

A move toward formalizing and documenting the standards and practices of the Desktop Development Group is vital to achieving these advantages. The goal is certainly not to lock down the PCs and force all development through a cumbersome bureaucratic process. The goal is to recognize different business environments and user needs, as well as different types of desktop tools, and provide some practical guidelines (and sometimes rules) to help everyone work and manage their work more effectively. The overall process is the system development life cycle, and the roadmap through that life cycle is the development methodology. We need a flexible map that takes into account whether we are using a bicycle or a truck and whether we are carrying a loaf of bread or a ton of bricks.

The Desktop Development Group is guided by the application spectrum (see Figure 7–2), which classifies applications according to their scope (single user to enterprise) and tools for user interface, processing, and data storage (for example, from Word/Excel to Java/Oracle).

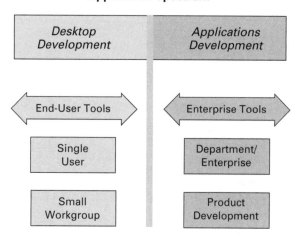

Figure 7–2 Application spectrum

The technological and business landscapes are always changing, with new information management tools and new business challenges appearing very frequently. As a result, the application spectrum is always changing too, and should be viewed as a flexible guideline rather than as a rule.

The Desktop Development Group generally focuses on solutions for the individual user and the workgroup, and also provides solutions in selected departmental and enterprise environments. In addition, the group is guided by specific elements of the locally required solution. The actual approach and tools to be used in any particular situation depend on many factors, including the specific business requirements, operating environment, resources, urgency, etc. So, like the application spectrum, these criteria should be viewed as flexible guidelines rather than as rules.

As shown in Figure 7–2, there is a "gray area" of overlap between the Desktop Development Group and the Applications Development Group, moving from higher end workgroups into the departmental/enterprise area. In this range of the spectrum, either group might proceed with development depending on the specific requirements and available resources, or a joint development effort might be appropriate.

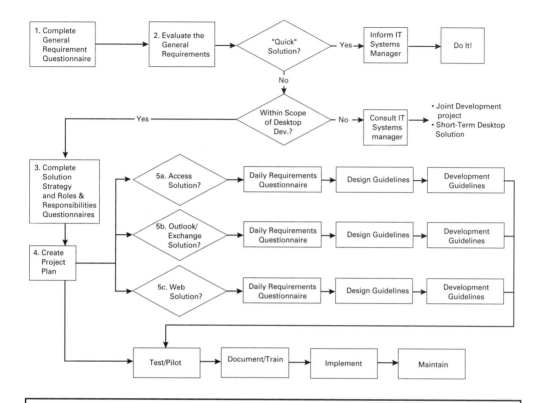

Desktop Development Top Nine List

1. Is Global IT informed of all actions?
2. Have you notified the IT Systems Manager?
3. Have you notified all areas of their involvement in the project (training, support, etc.)?
4. Does the Project Champion understand the responsibilities of that role?
5. Are you managing the scope of the project?
6. Have you identified all requirements and worked with the project champion to prioritize them?
7. Are you following the project lifestyle?
8. Are you managing your time to meet project milestones?
9. Do users understand the limitations of desktop tools?

Figure 7–3 Desktop Development Group's quick-start guide

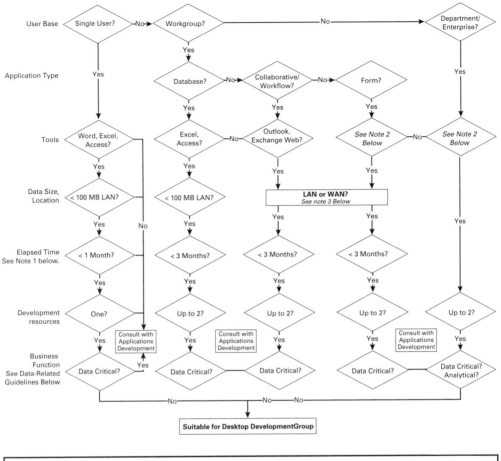

Additional General Guidelines	No analytical applications on a departmental or enterprise scale. No commercial product development.				
Data-Related Guidelines	*If the requirements include any of these characteristics, desktop database tools might <u>not</u> be appropriate:* • Data is highly critical. • Downtime is not permissible. • Transaction tracking or roll-back are required. • Record or field locking are required. • Extensive historical/time-keyed information is required. • Access to data in another system is required.				
Workflow Related Guidelines	*If the requirements include any of these characteristics, desktop workflow/form tools might <u>not</u> be appropriate:* • Replication is required for data that is updated in more than one place. • Complex automated routing is required Web-Related Guidelines.				
Web-Related Guidelines	*If the requirements include any of these characteristics, Web tools might <u>not</u> be appropriate:* • Form-based record browsing is the primary purpose of the solution. Note: Global Web/Internet infrastructure strategy is under development.				
Notes	1. Users generally deal in elapsed time or calendar interval between two dates when setting deadlines. It is difficult to estimate the amount of work time you will need to complete a project (i.e., actual time spent on planning, designing, coding, testing, etc.). When planning your project and managing expectations, be sure to take into account your work time for **all** the projects you are working on. 2. Desktop Development Tools: Word, Excel, Outlook/Exchange, and Web. 3. Size based on available data resources.				

Figure 7–4 Application suitability for the Desktop Development Group

The Desktop Development Group's thought process is best illustrated by an actual example, as shown in Figure 7–5.

Figure 7–5 Desktop Database Design Guidelines, Standards, and Procedures

People will frequently use a spreadsheet program to manage all of their information, but in many cases, the information would be better managed as a relational database. Using a database management system (DBMS) may seem at first to be more difficult, but when the information you're dealing with reaches a certain level of complexity, forcing it into a spreadsheet can be a losing battle. One reason a database seems "harder" is that there is another level of abstraction: Rather than putting all the data right there in front of you in a single table the way a spreadsheet does, the relational database uses a mysterious art called "normalization" to break the data into multiple tables, which then must be viewed through "queries" or reports. And when a database is structured (or normalized) properly, you'll need to link tables together to get any useful information. But once it is set up, assuming the information to be managed warrants it, a database is much more powerful, yet more flexible and efficient, than a spreadsheet.

In broad terms, a database consists of a series of tables, each representing a "real-world" object that the business deals with. Each row in a table represents a specific instance of the object, and the columns contain specific characteristics of that instance. For example, an Employee Table would have a row for each employee, and a column for each characteristic, such as ID number, First Name, Last Name, Address, etc. Tables are linked to each other through matching values in corresponding fields. See the sidebar for more information.

Naming Conventions

In general, each table and field name should meaningfully describe the object and should distinguish it from similarly named objects.

Relational Database: What's the Big Deal?

A common business situation illustrates some advantages of the relational database: Let's say you want to track employees (in a very small company). You might open up Excel, put in some column headings, and start entering data, one employee per row. You enter name (first and last in separate columns, right?), address (city, state, and zip in separate columns, too), and so on.

You're doing fine until you get to dependents. Some employees have none; most have one or two. You go through all your index cards and find that the most prolific worker has 5. So you put 5 columns in your spreadsheet, *Dep. 1*, *Dep. 2*, etc. Most of these cells are blank for most of the employees, and only one employee fills all 5, so there's a lot of wasted space in your file. Also, it probably won't be long before dependent number 6 comes along, forcing you to change your spreadsheet by adding another column, wasting even more space for all the other employees. Plus, all you

Figure 7–5 (continued)

have is the dependent's name; what about other dependent information you may need to manage?

In a relational database, you would still have your employee table, but it would have no information about dependents. Employees and dependents are two separate (but related) things, so they each get their own table. Your Dependent Table would have at least 4 or 5 columns: the employee's ID number, dependent's first name and last name (don't assume dependents have the same last name as the employee), probably date of birth, and maybe even full address (don't assume all dependents live with the employee).

As for the relationships between our "entities," how many dependents could an employee possibly have? Well, any number from zero on up. With a relational database, it doesn't matter. Each dependent gets his or her own record, no matter how many there are. The DBMS links the two tables by employee number: "Look at an employee record. Take that employee ID over to the Dependent Table and bring me all the records with the same employee ID." Now you have access to the employee, all dependents, and all of the information about them. In database lingo, you have a one-to-many relationship between the Employee Table and the Dependent Table and the employee ID in the Dependent Table is a foreign key.

Look at all of the additional dependent information you can manage in a database. If you'd added those additional columns (times 5 dependents) to your spreadsheet, it would be getting pretty large. And how about a new requirement: tracking the employee's work history? No problem—just add another table to the database. So a relational database is really a more realistic "model" of the real world, isn't it? That's the essence of data modeling and database design: Identify the things in the real world that you care about, identify the relationships among them, and then identify the characteristics of them. That's your database.

For more examples of the Desktop Development Group's thought processes, refer to Appendix C, "Desktop Development Standards and Procedures."

▶ Training Department Evolution

From the time a Training Department is created to the time when it becomes world-class (see Table 7–4), several issues need to be resolved. Among them are:

- ◆ **Documentation**—With each training class that is offered, there is an associated document. As new classes are offered, the list of documents increases. Documentation is not a one time only

Table 7–4 Evolution of the Training Function in IT

Initial Training Dept.	Enhanced Training Dept.	World-class Training Dept
Classroom instruction	Standardized instruction	Anywhere, anytime standardized instruction
Some documentation	Complete documentation	Documentation libraries
Training in macros	Writing complex macros	Coordination with the Desktop Development Group
Registrations	Automated registrations	Online registrations
Training at headquarters	Training in all offices	Distance learning
	Application training documentation	Standardized application training
	Global reporting	Global reporting
	Surveys and feedback	Surveys and feedback by business unit and region
	Demos, announcements, FAQ's	Demos, announcements, FAQ's, global schedules
	Function-based training plans	Function-based training plans for all job types

project since with each system enhancement or upgrade, documentation must be modified and enhanced. Therefore, documentation workload increases at a compounding rate.

- **Function-based training**—There is an increased demand for function-based training. Training courses provided are usually generic overviews, which introduce employees to the various applications, but do not necessarily show them how these applications can make them more efficient and effective.

- **Anytime/Anywhere courses**—Courses are typically offered once a month. Employees have demanding schedules, flexible work hours (telecommuters), and a high volume of travel. Training needs to become available to participants according to their schedules.

- **Online help files for in-house systems**—The Training Group receives requests to develop online help files for in-house systems. We expect these requests to grow with time.

- **Training plans for new employees**—Many employees are not sure which applications they will need to learn to effectively function in their job. Training plans are recommendations based on the new employee's job function as well as his/her department.
- **Accurate skills assessments**—Currently, when an employee doesn't know which "productivity" class to take, he or she will call the Training Group and ask for a recommendation. For in-house systems, there is no method to determine an employee's current skill level.
- **Realistic course evaluations**—To truly measure the effectiveness of the Training Group, course evaluations are needed for accurate measurement.

A good example of integration within the Personal Productivity Services Group is shown in Figure 7–6. It happens to be a page from a desktop development standards and procedures document.

Figure 7–6 Desktop Development System Training Standards and Procedures

---

Training

Training and documentation requirements are generally determined by the nature of the application (number of reports, transactions, etc.) and the number of system users. Be sure to review your user requirements with the training manager to determine the best approach to training and documentation. Training is also an important element in marketing an application. Scheduling and publicizing training courses can help to increase interest in the application and increase its utilization, as well as making the users more proficient.

Course and Documentation Development

For as few as 8 to 10 users the desktop training group will develop and deliver a training course for the application. For documentation, if the number of users is small (up to a dozen or so) a quick reference guide may be all that is necessary. For a larger number of users or a complex application, you may need to plan for a more complete user guide.

Timing

To develop training and documentation, the training group needs to get involved in your project when it is complete enough to be demonstrated.

Resources

For a training course, the users will need to provide business rules and/or a case study. Also, if the application involves a database, you will need to provide a nonproduction database for use in training sessions.

Figure 7–6 (continued)

System Administrative Tasks

Most desktop applications are designed with intuitive navigation (following windows conventions) and are so tailored to the users' operations that only minimal training in the application may be necessary in many cases. However, training and documentation may be required for system administration such as:

managing external data feeds (downloading files, loading floppies or CDs, converting data, etc.)

managing data backups and restorations.

Identify any such requirements and include them in your project plan.

Support

Be sure to include in your project plan notification to the help desk about your application and its scheduled implementation date. Also be sure to provide them with any necessary training and documentation for supporting the users.

Marketing

The project champion works with the training group to publicize a new application through e-mail announcements and training classes. These are effective methods of increasing awareness and use of the application. To maximize effectiveness, they must be scheduled carefully to coincide with the rollout of the application. The project champion may also publicize the application within the business unit with e-mail announcements, etc.

Implementation

Technical Standards

Implementation varies by tool: SMS, WINBATCH with .INI file.

All desktop development is designed for screen resolution of 800 x 600 and the standard Windows color scheme. All user workstations should be set to these properties.

Rollout plan

Your project plan should include detailed steps rolling out the application including any data conversion, desktop deployment, etc., activities that may be required.

A good example of how to be customer service-oriented and aligned with the business is shown in Figure 7–7.

Figure 7–7 Desktop Development Postimplementation Follow-up Standards and Procedures

Post-Implementation Follow-Up

After the new application has been operating for a while, it's time to step back and see if it is producing the results we expected. This is an often overlooked phase, but it is really one of the most important, since it's where we measure how closely we hit the mark with the project. It helps the business users judge whether they are getting the results they expected and thus whether this particular allocation of company resources was effective. And it helps IT in improving the development process.

It is a good idea to think about this phase at the beginning of your project. If you intend to measure changes in business unit performance, customer satisfaction, etc., after the new process is implemented, you'll need baseline measures from before it is implemented.

System Performance

Operational Measures

Production-type work is usually the easiest to measure, so it's the work that gets measured most. And it's easiest to see the affect of a new process or application. For example, let's say the month before the new system, the group processed 100 transactions per hour; 4 months after the new system was installed (allowing time for everyone to learn and get comfortable with the new methods), they processed 150 transactions per hour. Was that the productivity gain you expected? Is it larger or smaller than you expected? Why? If smaller, is there anything you can do to improve it? If larger, could other groups benefit similarly?

Doing a cost/benefit analysis early in the life cycle gives you a great advantage in doing these kinds of evaluations. The users should certainly know going in to the project what it is they want to accomplish, and how the results will affect their bottom line: Does that 50 additional transactions mean fifty percent more revenue? Does it mean the manager can reassign some of the staff to other responsibilities? And from a financial point of view, what is the return on investment in the new system? How long will it take for the increased revenue or avoided costs to pay back the cost of creating the new system?

Operational measures extend to the customers, too, particularly with systems that support them directly (common now with Web applications) or that support customer representatives (e.g., call center or order fulfillment applications). Customer surveys before and after implementation of the new process can demonstrate improved service and customer satisfaction.

Figure 7–7 (continued)

User Satisfaction

There is a lot to be learned by measuring how the users feel about the system. They are usually the best source for ideas on improving the user interface and on any bottlenecks in system performance, for example. A carefully designed user survey is a good way to obtain this feedback, and is preferable to user-initiated anecdotal "evidence." The former will generally give you a clear indication of any shortcomings, allow you to evaluate them in proper perspective, and thus set overall priorities for improvement; the latter may tend to emphasize the most negative aspects and lack perspective. Another source of information is records from the help desk. If patterns appear in the questions coming in from the users, it may indicate that, for example, some sort of educational remedy may be called for (e.g., a reference card, additional training, or even an e-mail to the users on how to avoid common problems).

Technical Measures

Any available technical measures, such as transaction volumes, table growth, etc., should be reviewed periodically to avoid problems such as running out of disk space. Plus, user satisfaction depends a great deal on system performance; as a system becomes more heavily used, you may need to consider moving it to a dedicated server, beefing up communication lines, etc.

Process Performance

The analysts and developers should take some time to look back at the project from the IT perspective, to judge how well the development process worked. Some questions to ask: Was your requirements gathering complete or did you have to redesign parts of the system? Were any players caught unaware of their responsibilities due to failure to communicate? Did you estimate your resource requirements and time line accurately? Did you learn more about how the business works so you can do a better analysis job next time?

For an overview of the mission, charter, and responsibilities of the Personal Productivity Services Group, refer to Appendix B.

HUMAN CAPITAL MANAGEMENT

As we've already said, our definition of the ideal IT environment is one that is designed to exceed the enterprise's strategic goals while nurturing the individual to achieve exceptional productivity and job satisfaction. This environment can be recognized by the following signs:

- Educated and committed enterprise executive management
- Complete alignment with business goals and objectives
- Strategic decisions that accommodate a rapidly changing, dynamic business environment
- Cost-effective
- Common architecture (i.e., tools, standards, etc.)
- Individuals blossoming instead of being buried in a bureaucracy
- A culture where honesty, mutual respect, and job satisfaction flourish

Emphasizing the individual and job satisfaction directly contributes to the achievement of exceptional productivity. Human capital management is the way we create and maintain this environment.

As IT moves from a cost center to a business partner, changes must be made to the way people are managed. This chapter will address the following areas of people management:

75

Table 8–1 Transitions from a Cost Center to a Business Partner

Cost Center Management	Enhanced Training Dept.
Autocratic, centralized decision making	Delegated responsibility and authority
Poor quality of life (overtime demands, unrealistic schedules, no budget for training, heavy travel schedules, moving staff from position to position without regard to person's aspirations, unrealistic job demands).	Quality of life (e.g., to to child's recital, enforced vacations). *People are valued as individuals.*
Technology as a job	Technology as a career
Staff Turnover (people issues are rarely considered)	Investing in staff in order to build effective teams operating in a synergistic culture: e.g., career paths, training, compensation planning, time off, staff retention, competent staff, low turnover, synergies, teamwork (built knowledge and experience as a team, training, mentoring, and investing).
Hire for technical competence only	Take the time necessary to make the right hire (career path, chemistry)
No career path	Career path/succession planning
People are taken for granted	Celebrate success
Budget for training not considered a priority	Training is always available (don't cut the training budget first)
Little communication	Common goals frequently reinforced. Personal ownership of enterprise goals. Frequent meetings at all levels. "I know what my management would do in this situation." Employer of choice surveys.

- ◆ Quality of life
- ◆ Recruiting and hiring
- ◆ Transitioning into the enterprise
- ◆ Mentoring for success
- ◆ Managing the process
- ◆ The organization as a career

Table 8–1 highlights some of the changes that occur as IT moves from a cost center to a business partner.

Quality of Life

Quality of life contributes to success. Quality of life is embedded in our values and is visible throughout our environment. The question to be answered is: "How do we create the appropriate quality of life and how does this environment create success for the business?" We have demonstrated how this environment creates business success and would now like to turn our attention to how to create the appropriate environment.

Quality of life is a combination of personal and professional satisfaction. Every individual seeks satisfaction and balance between his or her personal and professional lives. Each of us seeks respect, the ability to affect our environment, and the ability to grow both professionally and personally.

As we have seen, a management cornerstone is the delegation of responsibility and authority to the lowest possible level. Individuals must be both encouraged to accept responsibility and entrusted with the authority to carry out that responsibility. This delegation, along with overcommunication at all levels, leads to respect, control over one's environment, and growth, while fostering personal ownership of the enterprise's mission and goals. This sense of ownership and the discourse that is encouraged contribute to ideas of enormous operational and strategic value. It is not rare for policy decisions to percolate upward from the front lines. In fact, this should be encouraged. Delegation of responsibility and authority to the lowest possible level is risky. Most managers' instincts are to retain authority, even if they have been convinced to delegate responsibility. The introduction or appearance of introducing risk focuses management attention on the process and decisions being made, especially if everyone is being held accountable in a visible way.

Recruiting/Hiring

Quality of life is a strong recruiting tool. It separates the mercenaries from the technologists; bidding wars rarely land stable candidates. An equitable compensation package along with a desirable quality of life lead to long-term commitment and a dedicated employee. Compensation levels need to be kept consistent within the organization and should not be compromised, except under extraordinary circumstances. Your staff expects equity, and you owe it to them. Unbalancing the compensation structure to hire a new employee is nearly always counterproductive.

Use the interview process to build relationships. The process should allow the interviewers to get to know the candidate under unique circumstances. The candidate, under these unique circumstances (a shared experience), is building a relationship (or not) with each of his or her interviewers. When it is clear that a candidate is a potential employee, the interview process should be extended to include peers and business partners. This serves two purposes: It exposes a larger segment of the organization to the candidate and the candidate to a larger segment of the organization. The value is derived from the candidate's budding relationships, his or her understanding of the organization and its values, and the informal network he or she is building in the process.

Everyone in the organization needs to understand that immediate attention to an interview request is a very high priority. Interviews need to be scheduled rapidly and reliably. Interviewers need to recognize that they represent the firm every time they conduct an interview. Interviewing is an important responsibility and should be entrusted only to the most capable people. Annual performance measurement objectives need to include interview performance.

All potential interviewers need to be trained in interview techniques and the interview process. The interview process requires a strategy among the interviewers for each candidate; for example: Who will be handling technical questions; who will be asking redundant questions to get different perspectives; who will be questioning experience, etc. Interviewers should be exchanging thoughts while a candidate is going through the process. Interview results should be reviewed as a group; circulating interview notes is a good idea, but it is no substitute for a roundtable discussion of the candidate. This will give a complete view of the candidate and is an excellent learning experience for the organization. Issues about the organization can be addressed in these informal forums. It's also a good way of exchanging views in a noncontroversial way. After a few roundtable discussions, it becomes fairly easy to spot the right candidate, and during the process remind the interviewers of what they are all about.

Be grateful if the Human Resources (HR) Department wants to do initial screenings. By working closely with HR and allowing HR to handle recruiting firms and do initial interviews, the IT staff can avoid being overwhelmed by paperwork. As tempting as it may be to deal directly with recruiters, make certain that all recruiters are directed to HR. Don't confuse the process by allowing recruiters to speak directly to interviewing managers. If HR is not capable of doing this well, it should be an enterprise issue, not a reason for IT to be distracted from its main job.

Subordinate interviews should be limited to the final candidate. It is valuable for subordinates to understand that they have been part of the process, but it is risky to show multiple potential candidates to subordinates.

Take the time to hire well. There is rarely a higher priority than hiring the right person. It's better to be late with the right person than early with anyone else; spend as much time as necessary to get the right person. Never let the pressure of making a hire confuse you about a candidate's qualities. Never settle, but if you must settle, at least do it with your eyes open and plan accordingly. Not everyone needs to be a star, but everyone needs to fit a role and the organization. Compromising on candidate quality is occasionally necessary, but if left unchecked, it can lead to "negative synergy."

Compromising on experience is not necessarily a compromise. Experience can be learned, but attitude and intelligence are difficult to change. Attitude and intelligence outweigh experience.

The candidate profile will usually reveal whether or not someone is a "team player." This has become a cliché, but it can be boiled down to a single personality trait: the ability to submerge one's ego. This is also a trait of a good relationship-builder.

Candidates should rarely be hired only for the job for which they have applied. They should be hired for this position and the next two positions. In other words, they should be hired for a career. If a candidate is right for one opportunity and one opportunity only, the organization owes it to the candidate and to itself to make sure this is understood. If the candidate is satisfied with his or her limited career growth, it may be a good fit; however, if the candidate sees this differently, a problem could emerge.

▶ Transitioning into the Enterprise

Transitioning means making a smooth and successful placement within the enterprise. Investing in success means not only hiring well, but starting off on the right foot. It is the organization's responsibility to ensure a successful transition. This requires transition planning overseen at the senior management level, including attention to:

- Peer relationships
- Mentoring relationships
- Initial deliverables
- Initial presentations
- Meetings/task force participation
- Training plan

▶ Mentoring for Success

Transition planning leads directly to mentoring decisions. Every project leader has a mentoring responsibility. Mentors are responsible for ensuring the success of their charges. As we discussed earlier, our ethic is that everyone is responsible for everyone else's success. If someone is about to step into a pothole in the road, it is everyone else's responsibility to keep him or her out of the pothole or to pick him or her up after a fall. Mentoring is a more formal recognition of this and should show up in annual performance objectives.

Project leaders (and their managers) are responsible for accelerating the learning curve, teaching lessons learned, gradually increasing the delegation of responsibility/authority, encouraging the development of informal networks, continually giving feedback and advice, and constructing appropriate partner relationships.

▶ Managing the Process

At the center of recognizing quality of life, recruiting and hiring, transitioning into the enterprise, mentoring for success, and positioning technology as a career is the performance management process (PMP). Managing the process is more than cheerleading and requires formal objectives with scheduled reviews. Anything that is measured tends to improve. Taking stock of lessons learned, celebrating successes, actively managing career paths, and forming effective mentoring relationships need to be part of everyone's daily routine.

▶ Performance Management Process

Most firms have a PMP in place (see Figure 8–1). The details of the process are less important than the simple inclusion, as personal objectives, of the human capital management process we just outlined. This allows common goals to be frequently reinforced and a continuing evaluation of processes and people.

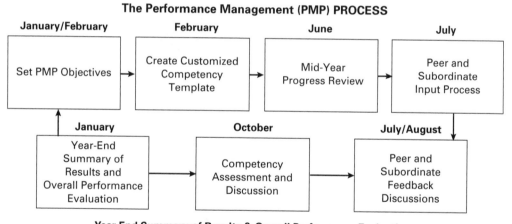

The Performance Management (PMP) PROCESS

January/February	February	June	July
Set PMP Objectives	Create Customized Competency Template	Mid-Year Progress Review	Peer and Subordinate Input Process

January	October	July/August
Year-End Summary of Results and Overall Performance Evaluation	Competency Assessment and Discussion	Peer and Subordinate Feedback Discussions

Year-End Summary of Results & Overall Performance Evaluation:

At year-end, actual results achieved during the year are summarized. This information is captured on the same form used to set objectives at the beginning of the year. Further, there is the option to add "additional accomplishments" that were not planned at the beginning of the year; however, the accomplishment is important to the overall assessment of the individual's performance contribution. In addition, the employee's overall performance evaluation, key strengths, development needs, and a development plan must be identified and added to the form.

The year-end PMP discussion is completed and then the PMP form is signed and sent to Human Resources.

Figure 8–1 Performance management process

Objectives at every level within the organization need to be consistent. From the CIO down to an entry-level employee, and from an entry-level employee to the CIO, all objectives need to flow smoothly and clearly.

Key points of a PMP include:

- Results-focused evaluation
- Evaluation measures achievement, not effort
- Overall performance ratings are reflective of the organization's overall growth for the year
- Evaluation is not a compensation tool

▶ The Organization as a Career

One result of this process is the positioning of the organization as a career rather than one's latest job. This leads to personal and organization stability. It builds continuity and self-confidence, but to succeed, it also requires commitment from employer and employee.

An example within the technology organization can be drawn from the Personal Productivity Services Group. If you recall, the Personal Productivity Services Group integrates support personnel and personal productivity applications at the desktop and individual levels. It is technology with a human face. It is composed of the help desk, first- and second-level support, training, and desktop development. By delivering these services through one organizational unit, support services are integrated in a very personal, visible, powerful, and synergistic way. The integration of these support services serves as a career growth objective as well.

At one company, the help desk was often seen as an entry-level position with rapid turnover. We observed this and recognized that a help desk staff member, properly evaluated during the hiring process, could move into a position in the Training Group, second-level support team, Desktop Development Group, or as a business analyst. In fact, all of this did occur. It is even fair to say that the integrated Personal Productivity Services Group may have come out of this realization as much as the understanding of the synergies inherent in providing an integrated service. An employee hired for the help desk, Training Group, or second-level support recognized the career growth afforded others in the organization who started in these positions. Not only did this allow the company to retain staff, but the continuity of knowledge within the Personal Productivity Services Group contributed significantly to its value within the enterprise.

INVESTING IN VALUES

Values are guiding principles, basic beliefs that are fundamental assumptions on which all subsequent actions are based. As a whole, values define the personality and character of an individual or group. Values are the essence of an individual or group and provide guidelines by which to make consistent decisions. In reality, values are ideals that are indicative of one's vision of how the world should work.

Appropriate values inexorably lead to principled actions and a high quality of life. They are a guide in hiring decisions, they establish a common culture, they foster strategic decision making (even short-term, tactical decisions made by guiding principles are strategic), and they lay the groundwork for internal consistency. Values form a contract between individuals and the group.

If all staff members are making decisions based on the same values, it is more likely that:

Delegation of responsibility and authority will function effectively.

Thousands of individual decisions will converge in a consistent strategy.

Synergies will be realized.

Partnerships will prosper.

Productivity will accelerate.

Retention will never be a problem.

The firm will reap large profits.

How We Succeed

Remembering the principles of consequence-based thinking from Chapter 2, we can now ask the question: "Why is it so hard to live below the line?" It is difficult to "live below the line" when guiding values are not given their D.U.E., that is, they are not adequately defined, understood, and embraced. As a result, the risk is too high to think beyond the situation, challenge norms, try something and fail, or admit to a mistake. What seems obvious is made impractical by an environment that feels like a river's current consistently running against you.

Let's take our model from Chapter 1 and reorient it vertically (Figure 9–1) to see how similar the two models are.

Giving values their D.U.E. becomes the secret ingredient that enables below-the-line actions to be executed on a consistent and sustainable basis. In essence, it redefines the flow of a situation and can actually change its direction (Figure 9–2)!

Values foster an environment where consequence-based thinking can thrive, but values alone will not guarantee below-the-line living. You need both skills and maturity to live below the line in every situation, and the values to ensure this expectation are supported by a culture that enables, rewards, and sustains these types of actions. Figure 9–3 shows another way to look at decision making using Chapter 3's operating principles.

Values

- **Loyalty is given and returned**—We all expect our employees to be loyal. By loyal, we don't mean the opposite of dishonest or treacherous, but rather we mean dedicated, considerate, and willing to make sacrifices. Loyal means seeing oneself as part of a team, believing oneself important to the team, and recognizing there is a team to be loyal to. Loyalty also implies responsibility to the team. Loyalty returned is the team recognizing its responsibility to the individual. If this is not acted on in concrete ways, it is meaningless. Every member needs to look out for the team, and the team needs to look out for every member.

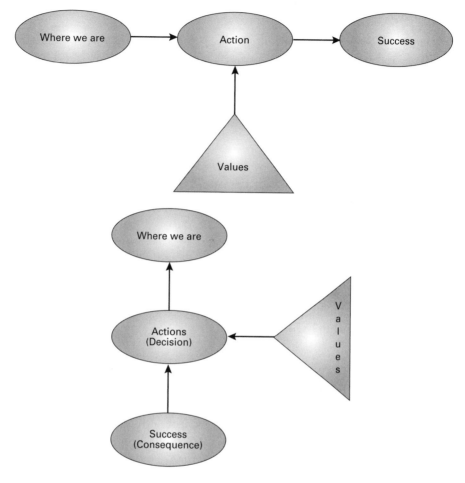

Figure 9–1 Investing in values (two models)

- **No surprises**—Adequate preparation requires overcommunication. Co-workers or partners should never be surprised by anything. This applies to peers, subordinates, and superiors. Differences of opinion should be worked out prior to any public meetings. It is everyone's responsibility to make sure no one is surprised—surprises lead to lack of trust, confusion, and personalization.

- **Mutual respect**—Mutual respect is required at all levels and with all partners. It is a manager's responsibility to assure that respect is both being given and returned. This is not always 100% achievable, but if not diligently pursued in visible ways, it

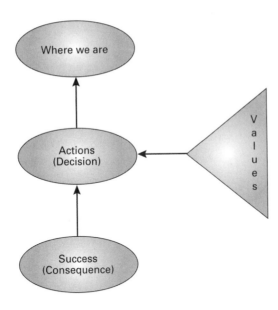

- Loyalty given/returned
- No surprises
- Mutual respect
- We are all responsible for
  each other
- Everything relates to an
  Enterprise objective
- See the world from your partners
- Honesty and candor
- Preparation & thoroughness
- Integrity
- Professionalism
- etc.

Figure 9–2 D.U.E.

will raise obstacles to effective execution as well as quality of life. However, respect must be earned and cannot be assumed. Never embarrass anyone. Not only is it not respectful, but it ruins relationships and trust.

- **We are all responsible for each other**—Every member of IT is responsible for every decision made by IT. This extends to IT business partners as well, though not as completely. If another member of the team (remember the team includes all partners, one of which is IT) is about to stumble, it is everyone's responsibility to either prevent the stumble or to steady the team member after the stumble. Within IT this is absolute. Whether or not a staff member has direct responsibility for an action, if he or she is aware of information that would assist another member or prevent another team member from stumbling, he or she is obli-gated to speak out. For example, if John is aware that while Jane is making the right decision, Jane will inadvertently surprise Tom, then it is John's responsibility to alert Jane to the potential surprise to Tom. If John remains silent and doesn't exert the effort to warn Jane, then John is not doing his job. Mentoring by John's manager or Jane's manager will ensure that both John and Jane learn this lesson.

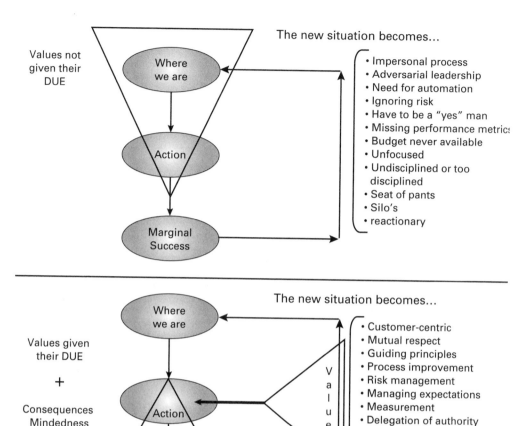

Figure 9–3 Decision making

* **Everything relates to an enterprise objective**—Without an enterprise point of view, nothing is strategic. A mission statement, while valuable, is not as useful as a set of enterprise objectives, which will achieve the mission. These enterprise objectives need to be given constant visibility. All significant projects should be matched against these objectives. All business cases should reference these objectives. A business case that earns profits but matches none of the enterprise objectives is suspect.

All strategic presentations should refer to enterprise objectives within them.

If enterprise objectives lack enough specificity to be useful in this manner, then the enterprise objectives need to be reworked. This is an enterprise problem and it's the CIO's responsibility to point this out.

- **See the world from your partner's point of view (anticipate all questions)**—Complete preparation requires anticipating all the questions you may be asked. You must not only anticipate, but have answers and understand the implications of your partner's questions. You may need to say, "Let me go away and figure this out," but it is far preferable to have anticipated and resolved issues in advance. You must be able to put yourself in your partner's shoes and predict his or her decisions. If you are presenting to your manager, you must similarly anticipate and answer his or her questions before they're asked.

    As your relationship with your partner matures, it can be measured by how successfully you've anticipated his or her questions and how often you've resolved them in advance.

    If you are frequently surprised by questions, there is an underlying problem, which must be discovered and resolved.

- **Honesty and candor**—It is surprisingly easy to be honest and totally lacking in candor. If you need to be asked the precise question to elicit the required information, then you are not doing your job. It is not enough to be honest in everything you say and do, but without being brutally frank, it is important to understand what is being asked and to answer with candor. Don't hoard or spin information. Be objective and make sure what you say is supportable.

- **Be prepared and thorough** (don't make a recommendation unless it is bulletproof).

- **Have integrity**—Your word must be absolutely and unwaveringly reliable.

- **Exhibit professionalism**—Be objective, knowledgeable, competent, dependable, reliable, thorough, disciplined, and well-mannered.

▶ Actions as a Result of Values

- **Delegation of authority**—Delegation of responsibility needs to be accompanied by delegation of authority. If an individual through inexperience or capability cannot be trusted to make a certain decision, then he or she shouldn't be given the responsibility to make that decision; conversely, if an individual is being asked to make a certain decision, then he or she should not need to seek multiple approvals before proceeding. There are decisions that need to be made quickly and confidently on the front lines. Authority needs to be delegated to the lowest practical level and not constantly second-guessed. The responsibility of the staff member making specific decisions is to understand what decisions he or she should be making and what decisions he or she should not be making. The goal of every staff member is to be able to predict what decision his or her manager would make in the same situation. Every manager should be mentoring his or her staff with the goal of delegating as much decision making as possible and being comfortable with the decisions being made. However, all managers need to clearly understand that abdication is not delegation. Ultimately, the entire team must take responsibility for all individual decisions. Mistakes become lessons learned.

  The stress level of an individual varies directly with his or her lack of control over the environment. Delegation of authority constitutes increasing control over one's environment, which reduces stress. The underlying assumption, of course, is that the individual has enough information and feels competent to make a decision in the first place.

- **Decentralized decision making**—While delegation of authority concentrates on individuals making decisions, decentralized decision making addresses organizational units making decisions. This requires all senior managers to share an enterprise-level view. It requires senior managers to understand and trust each other. It also requires a commitment to communicate both formally and informally. Senior managers are expected to make the distinction between putting their region first or chauvinistically considering only their region.

- **Mentoring as part of the culture**—Most management texts recommend that an individual looking to advance his or her career can best succeed by finding a personal mentor. This is good advice and not achievable by all who seek it. Mentoring as a shared value of the organization can achieve many of the benefits of a true personal mentoring relationship.

  The case of every individual within the organization should be reviewed annually at the senior management level to judge potential, career progress, additional/changed responsibility, training, and education (e.g., Master's degree, MBA, certificate programs, etc.). Many companies identify a group of people to be fast-tracked and give special attention to their careers. Mentoring has significant value beyond this narrow focus. While no organization can expect this fast-track level of mentoring for every employee, every organization should make mentoring part of its culture. Just as veteran baseball players take rookies under their wings, veteran technologists and technology managers at every level need to both formally and informally take responsibility for the advancement of all members of the group. During performance evaluations, mentoring should become a formal exercise; however, truly effective mentoring should be a continuous effort. Senior managers need to hold their subordinates accountable for mentoring.

- **Emphasis on relationships**—Good relationships are critical for good partnerships. Relationships need to be continually nurtured; relationships need to be institutionalized; and, relationships need to be grown beyond individual relationships to departmental relationships. The relationship must be viewed as value-added. A partner's perspective and needs must be anticipated. A good partner answers a question before it is asked.

  Relationships, while strongly encouraged on an individual level, need to be understood on a group level. For example, if a particularly difficult partner has been unable to form a relationship with the technology staff, the technology department must recognize this and take steps to forge the right relationship. This should require senior technology management to identify the sources of the relationship problem and proactively correct them. This may involve issues of competence, mutual respect, credibility, business knowledge and perspective, communications, etc. Relationships are not built overnight and require patience and consistency.

IT needs to review its relationships on a regular basis. IT partners/relationships depend strongly on senior management support. The tone is set at the executive or senior management committee level. Relationships are built top-down and bottom–up, but may not rise beyond a certain level in the organization without active senior management support. Sometimes a whispered word in the right ear works wonders.

Delegate relationships upwards, downwards, and sideways. Avoid jealously guarded relationships; they defeat the purpose.

A purchaser/contractor relationship is transitory and dependent on circumstances at a particular point in time. A partnering relationship encourages shared goals and objectives. Partners understand the need to accommodate because their relationship will exist beyond the current assignment. Partners do favors for one another and protect one another.

+ **The 80% solution is often best; don't aim too high or too low—** Don't let perfect get in the way of excellent. A recent study showed that 7% of requirements are all that is needed to completely specify version 1.0 of a product. Scope creep is probably the single biggest reason for project failure. While 7% may be difficult to recognize and enforce, 100% (or more realistically, 150%) is even more unrealistic.

Requirements are often given in terms of a solution. Asking questions about what is trying to be achieved rather than accepting a solution in the guise of a requirement is the first step to the right solution. Separating "need to have" from "like to have" is a difficult but necessary first task and should not be undertaken in an adversarial manner.

+ **It's not embarrassing to make mistakes (admit mistakes; never point fingers)**—Staff must be encouraged to admit mistakes and turn them into lessons learned. It must be pointed out that small mistakes can be easily rectified, but small mistakes, if hidden, are likely to turn into major embarrassments. Recognizing and correcting a mistake is something that deserves a pat on the back, not a slap on the wrist. It is the hiding of mistakes or the inability to learn from mistakes that requires a slap on the wrist.

+ Since we are all responsible for one another, it is never acceptable to point fingers.

+ **Don't confuse people with too much information (e.g., meetings, e-mails, memos, proposals, presentations)**—Clearly recognize the objective of your communication. If only the conclusion is necessary, don't clutter the communication with unnecessary analysis. If a line of reasoning is required, make certain that the conclusion is clearly stated and that the reasoning is succinctly worded and indeed leads to the stated conclusion.

Brevity and clarity are valued above all else. If there is a point to make, get to it quickly. If there is no point to make, don't waste anyone's time. Anticipate why the recipient needs the information and supply it in a manner to allow the recipient to meet his or her objective as simply and effectively as possible.

- **Be a good corporate citizen (sometimes doing things that aren't necessarily good decisions)**—Being a good corporate citizen requires an enterprise perspective. Not all decisions will be optimal for your particular group or business unit. If you are given the opportunity, make your case carefully, but recognize that while no one expects you to be totally selfless, no one expects you to be selfish either. Do not whine; embrace the enterprise perspective. (After all, you don't have a choice, so why damage relationships?)

  A track record as a good corporate citizen will entitle you to exercise more influence over enterprise decisions. There will even be times to make recommendations that are good for the enterprise and at the same time a sacrifice for your group. Always take a long-term view and value relationships above short-term convenience.

- **Never personalize anything**—Language tends to be highly personal, and even when a conscious effort is made not to personalize a statement, a comment can be taken personally anyway. All staff needs to be trained, mentored, and reminded to avoid personalizing comments and taking comments personally. Constantly reminding staff not to be defensive or adversarial and pointing out to them when they are is a neverending job.

- **Seek a solution; don't simply highlight deficiencies**—When approaching a problem, it is not appropriate to simply highlight deficiencies. Highlighting deficiencies is a negative endeavor and can be taken personally. Besides, everyone recognizes these deficiencies anyway. The correct approach is to craft a solution that gets everyone where they need to be. A positive attitude aimed at a better future is much more effective than picking at a weakness.

- **Don't hog the spotlight**—There will be many occasions when it is appropriate to allow your business partners to occupy the spotlight of success. It may be tempting to either hog the spotlight for yourself or your group. A mature partner relationship will avoid this situation; however, as the relationship matures, it is often appropriate to submerge one's (or one's group's) ego. Visibly getting credit is not nearly as important as a true partnering relationship. In the end, as this relationship grows, there will be more than enough credit to go around.

- **Recognize performance (a pat on the back never hurts)**—On an individual basis, we all need to know that our contributions are being recognized. Whether via a public pat on the back or a promotion, some form of recognition is always in order. The value of recognition should never be underestimated.

- **Don't build legacy applications**—Have a vision, have a strategy, and have an architecture. All applications should be built with an eye on the future and the flexibility to adapt and grow with technology. Nothing should be hardwired and everything should be modular. The objective is for no application to become a legacy application.

▶ The Hidden Harvest

We like to call the fruit that comes from successfully integrating guiding values into an IT organization the art of "reaping the hidden harvest." In more concrete terms, it means experiencing the rewards that working in synergy with others unlocks and experiencing potential gains that are in a different league and of a magnitude far greater than those achieved in the day-to-day process of just "getting the work done."

In a business context, this could mean:

- Growing a market rather than merely competing for a bigger share of the market.

- Unlocking gains that didn't exist before, internally or externally. These gains could mean efficiencies, leading-edge processes, reduced turnover, customer retention, speed to market, etc., all of which translate into earning more money, saving more money, or getting to market more quickly.

- Achieving that which no one has achieved before or that which would, to most, seem beyond their reach.

Achieving these kinds of breakthrough results requires that individuals, workgroups, and departments within an organization manage the coordination of many disparate entities, desires, and motivations. The level of coordination we are referring to can only come with individuals, workgroups, and departments that live the guiding values, values that enable them to achieve such lofty outcomes.

Living these values is key not only to being able to generate tremendous results, but also to feel good about how you achieve the results. The ability to feel good about the way results are achieved gives us the strength, continuity, and motivation to continue toward more success. Many companies achieve tremendous results, but are often unable to do so without significant costs to their people, which undermines the morale necessary to build the next successes.

Guiding values are the key to driving toward the synergy and alignment that unlock this otherwise hidden potential. Without guiding values, this potential might not only go unrealized, but unrecognized. Many organizations have no sense of what they are missing until a competitor leapfrogs them by unlocking this potential for themselves. By then, it's often too late and the organization finds itself responding to extreme external pressures and trying to play catch-up. Clearly, it is a focus on establishing guiding values that enables the alignment necessary to reap the hidden harvest and continue to lead in a competitive and ever-changing market.

The whole idea of reaping the hidden harvest is the fruit of consequence-based thinking, complemented by the guiding values that bring synergy, alignment, and a wide-reaching, clear sense of individual accountability for results across an organization. We are talking about the foundation necessary to engage in an enterprise that maximizes opportunity, not one that merely wins or beats the competition.

▶ Values of the Saturn Car Company

A well-known company that has put values to good use is Saturn. The following information can be found at *www.saturnbn.com*:

Values

- Commitment to customer enthusiasm
- Commitment to excel
- Teamwork
- Trust and respect for the individual
- Continuous improvement

Mission Statement

Earn the loyalty of Saturn owners and grow our family by developing and marketing U.S.-manufactured vehicles that are world leaders in quality, cost, and customer enthusiasm through the integration of people, technology, and business systems.

Results

In our first decade, we've sold more than 2.2 million Saturns. We believe there are ... basic reasons for our success so far... *we work as team members.*

The truth be told, most of us at *Saturn* didn't really set out to change the world. We set out to be honest and straightforward...

Our goals were to work together with people we liked and respected, to build quality cars at a fair price, and to offer excellent after-sale service.

We figured if we did that, people would want to do business with us. It worked ... The idea of good people working together is at the very heart of our approach to business. *And what works among individuals can work for institutions as well.*

CEO ROLES AND RESPONSIBILITIES

The CEO's job is to lead. Leadership means setting an agenda. A leader has a vision and sets the direction for the enterprise. The CIO's job is to supply the CEO's needs efficiently and allow the CEO's vision to be realized.

The CIO needs leadership from the CEO, partnership with the CEO, and education of the CEO.

▶ Leadership

The CIO needs to thoroughly understand the CEO's vision. If there is no clearly articulated enterprise vision, it is the CIO's responsibility to educate the CEO on the need for an enterprise vision and strategy. An enterprise technology strategy that does not relate to an enterprise vision is incomplete and difficult to sell. The technology vision process can lead to questions that provoke the creation of an enterprise vision; however, this is clearly not the most effective way to create an enterprise vision.

CIOs must always remember that successful IT executives need to consider themselves and convince others to consider them as part of the business, not separate from the business. CEOs need to understand that IT is mission-critical and needs to be managed as a strategic asset. It is inseparable from the business and requires complete alignment with the business goals. This understanding must be based on demonstrable evidence and constantly reinforced. It is the job of the CIO to demonstrate this fact to the entire senior management team. The CEO can be very supportive, but must play a strong leadership role in getting IT a seat at the table. CEO leadership should facilitate the creation of this partnership. Assuming the CEO believes that the CIO has the appropriate capabilities, the CEO needs to put the CIO on the executive/senior management committee and appoint the CIO to enterprise task forces. The CIO must be able to add noticeable value and earn the respect of his or her peers or this exercise will be fruitless. The CEO must support the CIO with the proper training and mentoring to assume these responsibilities.

▶ Partnership

Partnership with the CEO is important, but partnership with the senior management group is vital. The CEO can lead by example and facilitate the CIO's job; however, earning the support of true partners in the senior management group is key to professional success. The basic premises of this book have been the alignment of IT with the enterprise and the establishment of a partnership between IT and the business units. Success in these endeavors should allow the CIO to become a natural partner with the rest of the managers of the senior management group. It is the CIO's role to complete this natural cycle by establishing personal partnering relationships at the senior management level.

▶ Education

The CEO can support technology without becoming a technology expert. The CEO needs to understand the business case for IT as a strategic investment and to share the CIO's technology vision. It is the CIO's role to educate the CEO (and the entire senior management team) in the following:

- ◆ An enterprise vision is a prerequisite to a successful IT vision, and an enterprise strategy is a prerequisite to a successful IT strategy. It is the CIO's responsibility to educate the CEO on the need for both an enterprise vision and strategy.

- IT is mission-critical and needs to be managed as a strategic asset.
- IT is inseparable from the business and requires complete alignment with business goals.
- IT must be managed as an investment rather than a cost center.
- Business teams, including IT as a "business," must work together. Other than enterprise infrastructure, there is no such thing as an IT project. Whether IT is responsible for 10% of the tasks or 90% of the tasks, it is merely a member of a business team led by a business project champion.
- The CEO has a role in marketing IT. Marketing the IT organization increases the correct perception that IT adds value to the business. Marketing the IT organization raises the enterprise's recognition of its dependence on IT.
- Quality of life contributes to success.
- Values are the essence of an individual or group and provide guidelines by which to make consistent decisions.
- All projects require business unit champions and business project champions.
- All projects are required to build a business case; a technology case is not sufficient. All business cases are required to discuss the alignment of objectives with enterprise objectives.
- IT acts as a partner in the business since seeing its place in the success of the enterprise enables it to make decisions and put forward innovative suggestions that go beyond simply meeting the technical requirements requested by clients. Its ability to add value, if it has big-picture understanding and a big-picture mindset, increases dramatically in this environment.
- Value is best communicated to the enterprise by IT's business partners. The right relationship and recognition of value lead to the ideal situation of business partners becoming evangelists.
- The more meaningful an enterprise becomes to the individuals, the more effort people exert to bring about success.
- A strategic architecture has value.
- Alignment with the business needs to be more than a strategic plan or written set of operating principles. The technology organization needs to be set up in a way that allows business alignment to flow as a natural consequence of the way the job is done.
- CEO support is an active commitment.

Flying Solo

True success in the leadership, partnership, education (LPE) model means not only that IT has become a recognized and valued contributor to the success of the enterprise, but that the senior management team, including the CEO, can successfully represent technology on their own.

The Leadership, Partnership, Education Model

The three qualities of leadership, partnership, and education define the relationship of IT and the CEO. These qualities can be summarized and evaluated through the LPE model in Table 10–1. The columns represent the CEO's level of leadership to IT, partnership with IT, and education in the value of IT. The ideal row to occupy, of course, is the LPE row where the CEO is exercising leadership and partnership and understands the value of IT. It may be acceptable, though not optimal, for the enterprise to occupy either the OPE row or the LOE row. IT would need to supply strong leadership and rely on a strong partnership if it is in the OPE row. IT would need to concentrate on a strong partnership with other members of the senior management group if it finds itself in the LOE row.

Table 10–1 LPE model

L	P	E
0	0	0
0	0	E
0	P	0
0	P	E
L	0	0
L	0	E
L	P	0
L	P	E

SAMPLE BUSINESS CASE TEMPLATE

Project Initiation
for
<System, Version, Project Name>

▶ Document Overview

Document Purpose

The purpose of this document is to formally initiate a new IT project, <project name>. This document serves as a forum through which business and IT colleagues can formally, in clear, nontechnical terms:

- Describe what is being requested
- Define the scope of the project
- Explain why the project should be approved

- Set the criteria by which success will be measured
- Address any known risks
- Provide "ballpark" estimates concerning cost and time

This document is central to an agreement to proceed to the next project phase.

Document Amendment History

An overview of changes is listed below. For details of the changes, please refer to the relevant document section. The most recent amendment is at the bottom of the list.

Date of Change	Changed by	Change is in Section/Page	Description of Change
01-Jan-01	Mary Jones	Scope/6	Document created
16-Mar-01	Joe Smith	Requirements/10	Two new requirements added

▶ Project Summary

Strategic Rationale

This section addresses the benefits to be obtained from this project and/or the risks if this project is not completed.

Overview

In clear business terminology, briefly define this project by describing the product to be produced or the business problem to be addressed. Include anecdotal background information only if it is necessary to define the project. A brief discussion of the current business environment may prove helpful.

Action Steps

Define the high-level action steps required to complete this project. Examples:

1. Determine business requirements by <date>
2. Technical feasibility and architecture
3. New analytical process created
4. Completion of the new system by <date>

▶ Financial Summary

(in 000's <specify currency>)	<year> Est.	<year> Budget	Forecast		
			<year+1>	<year+2>	<year+3>
Operating Revenue	-	-	-	-	-
Costs and Expenses:					
Compensation	-	-	-	-	-
Consulting	-	-	-	-	-
Hardware/Software Maintenance (incl. software < 250K U.S. dollars)	-	-	-	-	-
Depreciation (3-year straight line)	-	-	-	-	-
Deferred Software Amortization	-	-	-	-	-
All Other Direct Expenses	-	-	-	-	-
Total Costs and Expenses	-	-	-	-	-
Net Operating Income	-	-	-	-	-
No. of Positions	-	-	-	-	-
Capital Expenditures (hardware, software>250K)	-	-	-	-	-
Deferred Project Costs	-	-	-	-	-

▶ Supporting Information

Project Team

Management Team

This section defines the senior management team (names, titles, and organizational units):

- IT Project Director
- Business Project Sponsor(s)

  Define project management (names, titles, and organizational units)
- IT Project Manager
- Project Champion

Extended Team

This section defines other (support) groups whose participation is necessary (e.g., Network Engineering, Operations, Database Administration, Quality Assurance, Auditing, etc.).

▶ Preliminary Requirements

This section should contain a detailed list of high-level functional and/or performance-related requirements. These requirements should tie into the previously stated goals and objectives.

Preliminary Project Scope

To provide context for the time and cost estimates that follow, the scope (scale) of this project must be clearly defined as it is currently envisioned within this section of the document. This may take the form of two lists: the first being functionality that is within scope and the second being functionality that is beyond the scope of this project.

Preliminary Time/Cost Estimates

This section contains further detail to support the estimated "Financial Summary."

Include verbiage that addresses the potential for error of the estimates that follow. In most cases, the necessary analysis and design will not have taken place to provide "firm" estimates. This should be stated. Furthermore, the people involved in compiling the estimates should be mentioned.

Major Project Tasks <only those applicable to this project >.

	EST. PERSON DAYS	EST. COST
Preliminary Analysis		
Systems Analysis/Design		
Programming		
Data and File Conversion Costs		
System and Program Testing		
Training Costs		
Hardware Purchase		
Software Purchase		
Administrative Costs		
Miscellaneous		
Total Cost		*<currency>*

Estimated Annual Operation Cost

Data Entry	xxx,xxx
Processing	xxx,xxx
System/Program Maintenance	xxx,xxx
Administrative	xxx,xxx
Other (specify)	xxx,xxx
Total Estimated Annual Operations Cost	xxx,xxx *<currency>*

▶ Other Considerations

This section contains preliminary discussions focusing on other issues applicable to this project (e.g., hosting, outsourcing, disaster recovery, possible "Request for Proposals," build or buy issues, etc.).

▶ Assumptions

Note any business, technical, or operational assumptions made when composing this document.

▶ Risks

An initial risk assessment is critical to the success of a project and forms the basis for a more comprehensive risk assessment at the end of the analysis phase. Review the following risks:

Risk Factor	Likelihood of Happening	Impact on Project
Unproven technology	H/M/L	H/M/L
Unclear user requirements	H/M/L	H/M/L
Issues with (lack of) business sponsorship	H/M/L	H/M/L
Issues with business management	H/M/L	H/M/L
Lack of skilled or available resources	H/M/L	H/M/L
Lack of control over critical resources (e.g., other IT groups)	H/M/L	H/M/L
Time-critical	H/M/L	H/M/L
Complexity of solution	H/M/L	H/M/L

List the actions that will be taken to mitigate the risk involved with any risk factor that has a value of high (H) or medium (M) in the "Likelihood of Happening" and/or "Impact on Project" columns.

Risk Factor	Required Action to Address Risk	Net Risk
Unproven technology	Describe action to address risk	H/M/L
Unclear user requirements	"	H/M/L
Issues with business sponsorship	"	H/M/L
Issues with business management	"	H/M/L
Lack of skilled resources	"	H/M/L
Lack of control over critical resources (e.g., NY IT)	"	H/M/L
Time-critical	"	H/M/L
Complexity of solution	"	H/M/L

▶ Sign-Off

This sign-off signifies the acceptance of this document and all contained within it.

Some form of sign-off is required, indicating the go-ahead to proceed from the business representative. If this sign-off is via e-mail, save the e-mail in a file and keep it with the project documentation. Recording the name, title, and date is also recommended.

Project Sponsor

Date:_____

Name: _____

Title:_____

Project Director

Date:_____

Name: _____

Title:_____

Factor	Calculation	Value
EXTERNAL DEPENDENCIES		
1. Are multiple vendors or major contractors/consultants involved in the project?	Yes = 2 No = 0	
2 Is vendor support (likely to be) poor?	Yes = 1 No = 0	
3. Are there any critical dependencies on external suppliers?	Yes = 2 No = 0	
4. Are there any inter-project dependencies?	Five+ = 5 Four = 4 Three = 3 Two = 2 One = 1 None = 0	
5. Is there overlapping scope with other developments?	Yes = 3 No = 0	
Total for External Dependencies		

Factor	Calculation	Value
ORGANIZATIONAL		
1. Are there multiple use areas or decision makers involved in the project?	Number of user areas and decision makers	
2. Are multiple geographical locations/implementation sites involved?	Number of geographical areas divided by number of implementation sites	
3. Do the users have any previous Information Systems project experience?	Yes = 0 No = 1	
4. What is the size of the user department/company involved? (How many people will be affected?)	Over 2000 = 5 1000–2000 = 4 500–1000 = 3 300–500 = 2 200–300 = 1 Under 200 = 0	
5. Are key users unavailable?	Yes = 5 No = 0	
6. Gauge the level of changes required to user procedures.	High = 3 Moderate = 2 Low = 1 None = 0	
7. Will users take joint responsibility for management and execution of the project?	Yes = 0 No = 3	
8. How much (user) education will be required to facilitate use of the new system?	Extensive = 2 A lot = 1 A little/None = 0	
Total for Organizational		

Factor	Calculation	Value
PLANNING AND SCHEDULING		
1. Is the project dependent on resources or skills that are scarce in the organization?	Yes = 5 No = 0	
2. Are the task dependencies complex?	Yes = 3 No = 1	
3. Is there a critical implementation date?	Yes = 5 No = 0	
4. Are formal project management control procedures being followed?	None = 5 A few = 4 More informal than formal = 3 More formal than informal = 2 Mostly formal = 1 Formal at all levels = 0	
5. Are there any major applications to be interfaced with?	Over two = 3 Two = 2 One = 1 Zero = 0	
6. Do any applications have an elapsed development time of more than 3 years?	Yes = 2 No = 0	
7. Do any applications have an elapsed development time of more than 12 months?	Yes = 2 No = 0	
8. What is the level of confidence of the team, the users, and the management in the schedule?	Most are < 85% confident = 3 Some are < 85% confident = 2 Most are > 85% confident = 1 All are > 85% confident = 0	
9. Has the project team agreed to key/milestone dates in the development plan?	Yes = 0 No =3	
10. How experienced is the project manager in managing projects?	Totally inexperienced = 4 1–2 small projects = 3 3–5 small projects = 2 3–5 large projects = 1 More than 5 large projects = 0	
11. Will planned resources be made available?	Yes = 0 No = 5	
Total for Planning and Scheduling		

Factor	Calculation	Value
BUSINESS CASE		
1. Are major increases in unplanned costs likely?	Over 20% likely = 3 10–20% likely = 2 5–10% likely = 1 < 5% likely = 0	
2. Are business requirements unclear/evolving?	Yes = 5 No = 0	
3. Are scope and requirements completely defined?	Yes = 0 No = 5	
4. Are benefits of the system well-defined?	Well = 0 Reasonably = 1 Badly =2	
5. Is this a mission-critical system?	Yes = 5 No = 0	
6. What is the level of commitment of the business to the development?	Very high = 0 High = 1 Moderate = 2 Low = 4	
Total for Business Case		

Factor	Calculation	Value
TECHNICAL		
Environmental		
1. Are the development tools appropriate?	All = 0 Some = 1 None = 2	
2. Is the technology new/unfamiliar?	Yes = 5 No = 0	
3. What percentage of the development team will remain throughout the project?	No change = 0 Over 60% = 1 41–60% = 2 21–40% = 3 11–20% = 4 1–10% = 5	
4. Is there adequate business knowledge on the project team?	Yes = 0 No = 1	
5. Gauge the IS skills of the project team.	Whole team expert or better = 0 Overall–Center of Excellence = 1 Overall–expert = 2 Overall–skilled = 3 Overall–inexperienced = 4 Overall–novice = 5	
6. Are development methods/standards being used?	Yes = 0 No = 2	
Project		
7. What is the complexity of the functionality?	All functions complex = 5 Most complex = 4 Most moderately complex = 3 Some moderately complex = 2 Most simple = 1 All functions simple = 0	
8. What is the complexity of the database (in terms of large numbers of entities/relationships)?	Complex = 5 Moderate = 2 Simple = 0	

Factor	Calculation	Value
TECHNICAL		
Environmental		
9. Is the development of the database to be shared by other, possibly undefined, applications?	Several undefined = 3 Several defined = 2 Few defined = 1 None = 0	
10. How many physical systems interfaces are there?	Over two = 3 Two = 2 One = 1 None = 0	
11. Are design documents clearly specified?	No = 3 Some = 2 Most = 1 Yes = 0	
12. What is the level of complexity of online networks involved?	Complex = 2 Simple = 1 None = 0	
13. Is this a multilevel hardware implementation?	Yes = 2 No = 0	
Operational		
14. Is upwardly compatible hardware available?	Yes = 0 No = 3	
15. What are the response time requirements (high = below 2 seconds)?	High = 5 Moderate = 2 Low = 0	
16. Is there high-volume throughput?	Yes = 3 No = 0	
17. What is the expected size of the database?	Very large = 3 Large = 2 Moderate = 1 Small = 0	
Total for Technical		

Risk Factor Category Summary

Project:		Date:

Phase:		

Project Manager:		

External Dependency Category		**Value**
Low Risk 0–4	Moderate Risk 5–8	High Risk 9+

Organizational Category		**Value**
Low Risk 0–5	Moderate Risk 6–10	High Risk 11+

Planning and Scheduling Category		**Value**
Low Risk 0–14	Moderate Risk 15–24	High Risk 25+

Business Case Category		**Value**
Low Risk 0–5	Moderate Risk 6–10	High Risk 11+

Technical Category		**Value**
Low Risk 0–11	Moderate Risk 12–30	High Risk 31+

Overall Project Risk Factor		**Total Value**
Low Risk 0–39	Moderate Risk 40–82	High Risk 83+

B

PERSONAL PRODUCTIVITY SERVICES ORGANIZATION OVERVIEW

▶ ## Desktop Development Group Overview

Mission

To provide software services that automate and improve business practices through the development of individual, workgroup, and enterprise solutions.

Charter

- Development of individual, workgroup, and enterprise solutions, managing the "full project life cycle"
- Prototyping and interim applications
- Expert consulting services
- Vision and direction for desktop technologies
- Third-level support
- Management services

- Third-party software
- Consultants
- Global coordination of desktop development solutions
- Software evaluation
- Global standards and methodologies
- Business partnering matrix (relationship management)

Benefits

- Rapid development
- Ease of use and supportability
- New functionality
- Productivity gains
- Global shared solutions
- Short-term solutions and prototypes
- Integration of workgroup solutions and larger systems
- Quality of "business life"
- Expert systems analysis available to everyone

▶ Training Department Overview

Mission

To provide enterprise staff with the necessary information to effectively use technology to make their work more efficient.

Charter

Represent Information Technology

- To represent IT, as we are often on the "front lines"

Training Administration

- Schedule classes, trainers, and rooms.
- Process course registrations, confirmations, reschedules, cancellations, and completed certifications.

- Request global schedules from other regions.
- Create and send global monthly training schedule.
- Set up and break down classrooms.
- Maintain rooms and machines.
- Maintain room schedules.

Benefits

Represent Information Technology

- All new employees have the opportunity to receive the same orientation.

Training Administration

- Anyone can take training anywhere in the world. If I'm traveling to Tokyo and I have a few hours available, I can take advantage of the classes there and learn the same information that I would learn in classes in New York.
- Rooms are maintained centrally—this reduces time conflicts and increases the integrity of the PCs.

Documentation and Training Development

- Create classes, courseware, and trainer notes to be used globally.
- Maintain documentation through upgrades, new requirements, etc.
- Duplicate documentation.
- Create documentation that will not be associated with a training course.

Documentation

- Make documentation that is branded, consistent, and easily recognizable.
- Create an agenda and handouts for every class. Solicit real-life examples from the business to make courses more applicable to everyday life.
- Create trainer notes for each standard course. Any trainer, anywhere in the world, can teach any course by following the

trainer notes. Trainer notes comprise a large amount of the operating procedures. Each set of notes comes with class files and exercises.

- Provide, whenever possible, the most recent version of the documentation.
- Provide user documentation for applications that require no course time.

Communications and Marketing

- Monthly e-mails and miscellaneous announcements (e.g., public folders).
- Types of announcements vary, as do the types of delivery media.
- Marketing announcements, promotions, presentations, and internal bulletins (for rollouts).

Training Delivery

- Provide classroom, remote, local office, and one-on-one training for most standard and newly developed applications.
- Deliver timely and effective software instruction and technical training.
- Pilot new courses for the help desk. Make changes to courses as necessary.
- Deliver anytime, anywhere training and training on different types of media.

Communications and Marketing

- User community is aware of upcoming changes to technology.
- Standards are created which, when followed, guarantee that messages are: (1) easily understood, and (2) complete.

Training Delivery

- Training goals are globally consistent. The length of a course may vary from office to office or region to region, and the examples used in class may also differ; however, students receive the same knowledge from a particular class regardless of where the class is held.

- Pilot new courses for the help desk. Make changes to courses as necessary.
- Deliver anytime, anywhere training and training on different types of media.

Miscellaneous Tasks

- **Statistics**—Gather, analyze, and report on training locally, regionally, and globally.
- **Rollouts**—Facilitate the rollout of new and/or upgraded software. This includes determining/documenting configurations, communications and marketing, and (of course) training.
- **Presentation support**—Provide presentation guidance and support as well as facilities.
- **Statistics**—Look for global, regional, and local trends. For example, if no one is signing up for a course anymore, that course should be retired. Also, statistics are a vehicle to use in communicating information about new courses taught in each region. For example, say that HTML was recently taught in Tokyo. If there was a need to teach that course in an office in the Americas, we now know that the course exists.
- **Rollouts**—Act as a user advocate, making sure that custom configurations will be easily accepted and incorporated.
- **Presentation support**—Use expertise in presenting to help others within IT.

Documentation and Training Development

- Although improving, notification of new applications is often last-minute.
- The tasks associated with creating a training program are usually not recognized, known, or understood.
- Trainers are often not treated as professionals.
- Documentation is never finished.

Communications and Marketing

- This is a relatively new responsibility and not adequately resourced or budgeted for.

- Internal IT marketing and communications are on a per-project basis. Communications within IT need to become more regular.
- People expect richer information—we need to bring our skills up to par to meet this requirement.
- Time is an issue.
- Once is not enough.

Training Delivery

- Trainers are also on the front lines.
- There is never enough time to provide training to everyone who needs it (regionally).
- Training trips are great time hogs in terms of preparation and delivery.
- Trainers cannot keep up with the demands for more technology-based training.

▶ Help Desk

Mission

To sustain business growth by providing employees with a single point of contact for coordinating and resolving technical and nontechnical computer requests.

Charter

- Resolve technical support requests on first call.
- Route, escalate, and ensure resolution of all support calls forwarded to other IT staff.
- Perform ad hoc one-on-one training.
- Provide technical and nontechnical administration.
- Facilitate information flow between IT staff and user community.
- Communicate IT policies and procedures.

Sample Help Desk Customer Service Survey

It is very helpful to gain feedback through a customer survey. The following example is a bit lengthy, but it has worked very well in practice.

Information Technology Survey 2001

Thank you for taking the time to complete this survey. When you have completed the survey, click the "Submit" button at the bottom of this document to send it to the Information Technology Group. Your survey remains anonymous unless you enter your name into the "Optional" section.

Instructions

To answer a question, click in the radio button under your choice. To move to the next question, press Tab on your keyboard. When finished click the "Submit" button or press Enter on your keyboard. For example, "Very" satisfied is selected below.

Extremely	Very	Somewhat	Not very	Not at all
○	○	○	○	○

If you are "Not very" satisfied or "Not at all" satisfied, please type your reason into the associated "Comments" text box. We would also appreciate it if you would enter your name, so that we can call you to discuss your issues further. Likewise, if you are "Extremely" satisfied, also let us know what we are doing right by filling in the "Comments" box.

Asia-Pacific Information Technology (IT) Support Services Charter

Your local IT staff, with regional and global support, coordination, and standards, carries out the IT support service.

The objectives of Information Technology Support Services are to:

- Provide effective, responsive help desk support to users.
- Provide training to users in IT applications and systems.
- Support, design, and implement business applications and systems solutions to address user and business requirements. Maintain and enhance IT systems (network, servers, personal computers, Windows NT, Word, Excel, PowerPoint, e-mail, printing) to provide a function-rich, reliable, and robust IT platform to optimize staff productivity.

SECTION 1—Asia-Pacific Help Desk

SERVICE QUALITY OF THE HELP DESK PROCESS

1. How satisfied were you with the service you received from the help desk (your local IT staff) in each of the following areas?

	Extremely	Very	Somewhat	Not very	Not at all
a) The willingness of IT to listen to your opinions	○	○	○	○	○
b) Overall understanding of your problem or inquiry	○	○	○	○	○
c) Effectiveness in communicating the resolution or resolving the problem	○	○	○	○	○
d) Professionalism of IT staff	○	○	○	○	○
e) Hours of help desk operation: Hong Kong 9:00 a.m. – 5:30 p.m. Melbourne 8:30 a.m. – 6:00 p.m. Tokyo 9:30 a.m. – 5:30 p.m. Singapore 8:30 a.m. – 5:30 p.m.	○	○	○	○	○

Comments

RESPONSIVENESS OF THE HELP DESK

2. How quickly were you contacted by the help desk (your local IT staff)?

Within 2 hours	Within 4 hours	The same day	Next business day	2 or more business days	Not contacted	Don't know/Remember
○	○	○	○	○	○	

3. From the time the help desk (your local IT staff) was first contacted, how long did it take for the problem or inquiry to be fully resolved?

Within 2 hours	Within 4 hours	The same day	Next business day	2 or more business days	Not contacted	Don't know/Remember
○	○	○	○	○	○	

4. Was the amount of time from when the help desk (your local IT staff) was first contacted to final problem or inquiry resolution?

Shorter than expected	About right	Longer than expected	Not yet resolved	Don't know/Remember
○	○	○	○	

Comments

CONTACTING THE HELP DESK

5. Based on the following methods of contacting the help desk (your local IT staff), how satisfied were you with the response received? Also, which is your preferred method of contact (most preferred method = 1; least preferred method = 3)?

	Extremely	Very	Somewhat	Not very	Not at all	Order of preference
a) Phone call	○	○	○	○	○	
b) Voicemail	○	○	○	○	○	
c) E-mail	○	○	○	○	○	

Comments:

OVERALL SATISFACTION WITH THE INFORMATION TECHNOLOGY HELP DESK

6. Taking into consideration your above answers, how satisfied were you overall with the help desk (your local IT staff) service?

Extremely	Very	Somewhat	Not very	Not at all
○	○	○	○	○

Comments:

DO YOU ASSIST YOUR COLLEAGUES?

7. Do you find yourself providing assistance to your colleagues in the use of computer applications and systems?

Yes ▣ No ▣ (If No, please skip to Question 8.)

a) How many minutes per week on average do you spend providing assistance? ☐ 0

b) Please provide details about the type of assistance you provide.

SUGGESTIONS FOR IMPROVEMENT OF THE HELP DESK

8. Did you encounter any problems or did you have any concerns in your most recent contact with the help desk (your local IT staff)?

Yes ▣ No ▣ (If No, please skip to Question 10.)

9. Can you explain what the problem or concern was and whether it was resolved by the help desk (your local IT staff)?

10. Please tell us, in order of priority, what IT could do to make you more satisfied with the IT support you receive from the help desk (your local IT staff)?

a)

b)

c)

d)

SECTION 2 — Training

1. How satisfied are you with the training programs provided in the use of IT applications and systems?

Extremely	Very	Somewhat	Not very	Not at all	Did not attend
○	○	○	○	○	

Comments/Suggestions:

2. Are there any applications that you believe IT could be providing training for but currently are not?
If so, please list below:

a)

b)

c)

d)

Sample Help Desk Customer Service Survey   125

SECTION 3—Application Development and Support

1. How satisfied are you with the support provided and the performance of the following S&P developed applications?

	Satisfaction with Support						Satisfaction with Performance	
	Extremely	Very	Somewhat	Not very	Not at all	Do not access	Satisfactory	Unsatisfactory
a) Access databases	○	○	○	○	○	○		
b) Word macros	○	○	○	○	○	○		
c) Excel macros/templates	○	○	○	○	○	○		
d) CARD	○	○	○	○	○	○	○	○
e) Classic	○	○	○	○	○	○	○	○
f) CMAP	○	○	○	○	○	○	○	○
g) CORE	○	○	○	○	○	○	○	○
h) Corporate toolbox	○	○	○	○	○	○	○	○
i) FIDO	○	○	○	○	○	○	○	○
j) Global sector review	○	○	○	○	○	○	○	○
k) PMP competency assessment (in Internet Explorer)	○	○	○	○	○	○	○	○
l) WFM	○	○	○	○	○	○	○	○
m) LinX	○	○	○	○	○	○	○	○
n) Direct	○	○	○	○	○	○	○	○
o) Remote	○	○	○	○	○	○	○	○
p) SOE security disclosure	○	○	○	○	○	○	○	○
q) SPIDI	○	○	○	○	○	○	○	○
Melbourne Only								
r) Subscribers database	○	○	○	○	○	○	○	○
s) Wanda	○	○	○	○	○	○	○	○
Other (please specify)								
	○	○	○	○	○	○	○	○
	○	○	○	○	○	○	○	○

Comments/Suggestions:

2. Have you identified any application requirements for your office and/or changes/enhancements for existing applications? Please specify below. (Please ensure that you provide your name also so that we can follow up on your requirements.)

SECTION 4—Information Technology Systems

NETWORK ACCESS

1. How satisfied are you with access to the following systems?

	Extremely	Very	Somewhat	Not very	Not at all
a) E-mail services	○	○	○	○	○
b) File access (network drives, e.g., E and F drives)	○	○	○	○	○
c) Office 2000	○	○	○	○	○
d) Internet/Intranet	○	○	○	○	○
e) Printing	○	○	○	○	○

Comments/Suggestions:

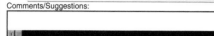

COMPUTING EQUIPMENT

2. How satisfied are you with the computing equipment you use?

	Extremely	Very	Somewhat	Not very	Not at all	Do not use
a) PC/Notebook	○	○	○	○	○	
b) Printer(s)	○	○	○	○	○	
c) Pool notebooks	○	○	○	○	○	○
d) Data projector	○	○	○	○	○	○

Comments/Suggestions:

REMOTE ACCESS

3. How satisfied are you with the services/tools used for accessing e-mail and network files remotely?

	Remote Access from Home					Remote Access When Traveling				
	Extremely	Very	Somewhat	Not very	Not at all	Extremely	Very	Somewhat	Not very	Not At All
a) Using remote	○	○	○	○	○	○	○	○	○	○
b) Connection success	○	○	○	○	○	○	○	○	○	○
c) Connection reliability	○	○	○	○	○	○	○	○	○	○
d) Connection speed	○	○	○	○	○	○	○	○	○	○

Comments/Suggestions:

continue...

continue

OTHER

4. Do you have any particular problems, requirements, or areas for improvement with the IT systems that you would like to see addressed?

Thank you for your cooperation!
Click the "Submit" button below to submit your survey.

Submi

Please provide your name if you would like us to follow up on any of your concerns.

Optional

Name:

Position:

Location: -- Select Location --

▶ Technical Support

Mission

To sustain business growth by providing employees with efficient, professional, and courteous hardware management and support.

Charter

- Create hardware standards.
- Create and maintain images.
- Provide hardware management.
- Manage assets.
- Maintain vendor relations.
- Coordinate staff relocations.
- Set up new laptops and support existing ones.
- Install and troubleshoot printers.
- Support the help desk.
- Provide hardware support.
- Coordinate the replacement of defective equipment.
- Participate in IT projects.
- Provide telecommuting equipment.

- Provide support to other coordinators and staff.
- Deploy new PCs to new hires and replacements.

▶ Second-Level Support

Mission

To remove technical obstacles to productivity and sustain business growth by efficiently delivering advanced technical support to meet clients' needs and deadlines.

Charter

Services we provide to the business:

- Technical customer service
- Ad hoc one-on-one training
- Information and recommendations for technical solutions
- Advanced administration

Services we provide to IT:

- Visit company offices.
- Conduct technical interviews for software services candidates.
- Support for the help desk.
- Identify opportunities for IT to create standards.
- Cross-train IT members.
- Participate in team projects.

Benefits

- Clients focus on their work rather than computer problems
- Less downtime = less stress for clients
- Instant training allows clients to continue to work seamlessly
- Research and recommendations of new tools to provide an optimal environment
- Cost savings

▶ Applications Architecture Overview

Mission

To support application development project teams by:

- Managing the application infrastructure
- Providing resources to augment project teams
- Planning technology
- Building methodologies and tools

Charter

To partner with business units and enterprise teams to improve the efficiency of the development process by:

- Identifying best practices and leveraging technologies for multi-business unit applications
- Using tools to support the project lifecycle
- Facilitating the documentation of standards and procedures
- Sharing information: results of design reviews, technical discussions, vendor bug reports and white papers, document enterprise objects, etc.

Forms of Engagement

- Design review
- Limited to design; not actively part of project/build plan
- Outcome of design review documented for future use
- Critical in cases where projects are deployed on "shared platforms"

- Problem resolution
- Provide expertise to resolve critical production or development issues
- Engagement limited to solving a specific technical issue

- Partially deployed resource as member of project team
- Engagement has fixed time
- Engagement is limited to proof-of-concept phase of project, and should not be included in project plans for build phase
- Resource reports on dotted line to project manager
- Project team partners in proof-of-concept; all knowledge transfer completed when architecture team resource rolls off project

- Fully deployed resource as member of project team
- Engagement has fixed time
- Engagement includes proof-of-concept phase of project
- Resource reports on dotted line to project manager
- All knowledge transfer completed when architecture team resource rolls off project
- Technology planning

- Strategic planning for use of technology
- Partner with infrastructure to set directions for platform and application infrastructures

Roles of Architecture Group

- Technology enablers
- Technology strategists
- Standards and guidelines
- Reusability among applications
- Components library
- Design reviews
- Design patterns
- Jump-start projects
- Tools and technology selection
- Capacity planning
- Mentoring
- Lessons learned
- Maintaining vendor relations
- Maintaining software library

▶ Architecture Group Involvement

- Start at planning phase of new initiatives.
- Plan resources for architecture/design needs.
- Involved in choosing tools and technologies.
- Make architectural decisions.
- Conduct design reviews.
- Develop software development methodology.
- Design system and database.
- Ensure reusability (enterprise objects).

Desktop Development Standards and Procedures

▶ Project Lifecycle

Desktop development policy is to follow every step in the project lifecycle for all projects except "quick solutions." The actual deliverables produced in each phase will vary, based on many factors, including the scope and complexity of the system, the technology used, IT resources required, experience of the user community, visibility of the project, etc. For example, a simple Access application targeted at one or two experienced users may not need as much user documentation and training as a more complex system or one aimed at less sophisticated users. However, on every project, you need to think about documentation and training, consult with your manager and colleagues, and document your strategy, whether it is large or small. Then, validate your proposal with the users and come to an agreement on an approach. Go through this basic process for every phase in the lifecycle.

Request Management

The objective of request management is to identify a user need or opportunity for information management technology, find out at a high level what the requirements are, and start to identify some possible solutions to the request, again at a high level. The result of this step is a determination as to what the next step should be.

Gather High-Level Requirements

You'll need to identify the person and/or organization making the request, and get a general idea of what it is they want to accomplish. This should help you estimate the scope of the project and develop some ideas about possible solutions and their relative feasibility. You'll also need to weigh the resource requirements both within IT and on the user side. The application spectrum provides guidelines on whether a project falls under the mission of the Desktop Development Group, or should be forwarded to the Applications Development Group.

Notifications

Whatever the disposition, the request should be distributed to the user and IT communities.

- Use the Business Partnering Matrix as your guide for identifying the business and IT people who will be involved in your project and document them on the "Roles and Responsibilities" questionnaire. Your "General Requirements" questionnaire and "Solution Strategy" questionnaire together document the need of the business unit and what action the Desktop Development Group should take to meet that need. Management involvement is necessary to ensure that the request is coordinated with other current and planned activities in the user area, and to ensure that the appropriate managers understand their responsibilities.
- Distribute to the IT community a document of what resources will be needed. This can be used to provide planning information to other organizations (training, support, etc.).

Best Practice:

Follow EVERY step in the project lifecycle!

Use the lifecycle as a checklist and consult with your manager and colleagues to plan each phase. Document your rationale for your approach and make sure the users agree. Then, notify everyone involved in the project.

▶ Requirements Gathering and Analysis

For a request that requires more than a "quick solution" (more than, say, a few hours of effort), you may need to do some more work with the users to find out what the requirements are and devise a solution. The essential purpose of this phase is to identify clearly and unambiguously what the users' requirements are, to communicate that understanding back to them, and to obtain their concurrence that you understand. If you're going to enter into a contract to build a solution, there must first be a meeting of the minds.

Depending on the scope of the opportunity, you may be able to get all the information you need with a few phone calls or meetings, and record it with a few paragraphs of narrative and some screen prototypes. Or, some tools lend themselves to the "build, expand, and refine" method, where the application and requirements evolve together.

As projects get larger (particularly if more than one developer is involved), you may need to use some of the more traditional tools and techniques for documenting the operations of the business area and identifying requirements. This section presents an overview of some of these tools and techniques; it is not intended to be a course on how to use them.

Requirements gathering and analysis can have these results:

- You may discover a solution that you can put into place without a formal plan/design/develop process.
- You may determine that while the solution is more involved, it still falls within the charter of the Desktop Development Group, and you have a good idea for a feasible solution. Your next step will be project acceptance, where you'll formalize your understanding of the requirements and your proposed solution, and develop the project charter with the users. Then it's on to project planning, design, and development.
- You may find that after getting more details, the project is beyond the scope of the Desktop Development Group. In this case, you'll want to coordinate a hand-off to the Applications Development Group.

Whatever the result, you will need to communicate it to the user community and within IT.

Role Definition/Notification

The Business Partnering Matrix is your guide to identifying the people who will provide information on the requirements, and who will need to be informed about your activities.

Gathering Application Requirements

After identifying the people who will provide information, you will need to determine the best methods of recording and communicating the requirements information you collect. Key points to remember are:

- The techniques should reflect the information rigorously and unambiguously.
- Documents must truly be understandable to the users—not necessarily at first sight, and not necessarily without some explanation of, for example, diagramming conventions, but informed consent requires true understanding.

The second point does not mean "dumb it down." The users do know their business. It's your job as an analyst to demonstrate that you know their business too, and to help them understand exactly how your technical solution is going to do the job for them.

Diagrams

Diagrams are very helpful for communicating how a business area operates.

Narrative

Plain old prose is probably the most frequently used tool for capturing requirements. The challenge for the analyst is that the two basic goals (to be rigorous/unambiguous and understandable) are often at odds with each other. The familiar composition rules of outlining, organizing logically, and writing simply (along with including some diagrams) are helpful.

Similar Applications

It may be helpful to show the users some existing similar applications to help them understand and communicate their requirements.

Cost/Benefit Analysis/Feasibility Study

Usually, the benefits of improved information management so far outweigh the costs that the wisdom of proceeding is self-evident. In some cases, particularly for a large-scale system, you may be called on to do a formal cost/benefit analysis. You may need to provide assistance to the users in documenting the tangible and intangible benefits of a new process. Benefits generally consist of some combination of increased revenue, avoided costs, and improved service. It may be useful to do a return-on-investment analysis to justify a large expenditure. A difficult part of cost/benefit analysis is to assign a real value to intangible benefits. You can usually find some tangible effect for an intangible benefit; for example, you know that new screen designs would just look better, but a tangible benefit might be that improved morale should result in X more transactions per day being processed.

In any event, information you gather about the current state of affairs will be valuable later when you want to measure the effect your project had on the business.

User Priorities

A benefit of this exercise is for the users to understand the true costs of application development, and understand their priorities for improving their operations, both within the requesting unit and in relation to other business units.

IT Resources and Costs

On the IT side, be sure to include all development costs, hardware (servers, routers, disk drives, etc.), and system software (operating system licenses, database management system software, development tools, etc.), as well as other resources such as training, documentation, and support.

Best Practice:

Show examples of existing applications.

To help the users understand and articulate their requirements, it may be helpful to discuss or show examples of similar applications. The users may see useful capabilities they were not aware of, or different approaches to their problem they may not have thought of. Plus, you may find an application that can meet their needs with little modification.

▶ Project Acceptance

Project Charter

In this phase, you will develop a project charter. This document formalizes the agreement between the Desktop Development Group and the users to proceed with the design and development of the solution. The project charter includes:

- A summary of the requirements you documented in the previous phase
- An overview of your solution, including all major components: the platform/technology to be used, an estimate of development time and resources, and identification of training, documentation, and support that will be required
- An overview of the activities that will take place from now through system delivery and implementation (bullet points from the project plan template)
- A discussion of scope freeze
- The date by which the overall project plan (if any) will be published
- Signatures of the appropriate managers of the user organization

Approval/Communication

- Distribute to the user community using your "Roles and Responsibilities" questionnaire as a guide.

- Distribute to the IT community to notify them that the project plan will soon follow with more specific information on what their involvement will be and when they will be needed.

Best Practice:

Discuss scope freeze early and often.

Frequently, once a project is underway, additional requirements and change requests begin to appear. These requests can quickly get out of control and threaten project milestones, and sometimes even threaten the entire project itself. This is referred to as "scope creep." The Desktop Development Group's general practice should be to implement a scope freeze before the development phase begins. However, depending on the complexity of the project, it may be necessary to freeze earlier, or not at all. In any event, it is important for the users to understand as early as possible if and when the freeze will occur.

Scope creep is a key reason why the requirements gathering phase is so important. When all of the requirements have been documented, the users can set priorities to make sure the most important features are implemented first, and other features are implemented in later releases. This helps everyone plan, design, and manage more effectively.

▶ Project Planning

The project plan is the master list of tasks, resources, and dates for accomplishing the goals of the project charter. The actual activities for any particular project are determined by the business circumstances, the type of application, and to some extent, the development tool. A project plan is important because:

- It serves as a checklist of all steps in the process.
- It is an effective way to communicate resource requirements and project status.
- It helps the users understand the development process and their involvement in it.

Always complete your solution strategy as the first step in your project planning. Then, consult with your manager to determine whether additional detail is required based on project scope and other considerations.

Project planning involves the following activities:

List Phases, Activities, and Tasks

- Think through each step required to create the solution and get it into operation.
- Group steps logically.
- Estimate dates.

Identify Resources

- Users
- Developers
- Training/Support
- Desktop deployment
- Help desk
- Marketing
- Other

Publish the Plan

- To business organizations
- Within IT

▶ Design

In system design, you will create a comprehensive system model or specification that:

- Demonstrates the application's user interface and flow
- Specifies the programming logic/algorithms and data structures

The basic objective is to capture in some tangible form a detailed description of what you propose to build. The design can then be reviewed and refined if necessary until the users agree that the application will meet their needs, and the IT people agree that the system is technically feasible and practicable. Design documents generally include narrative descriptions of data sources, processes, and outputs, plus diagrams illustrating these system features. Another tangible representation of the system could be a prototype. A prototype can demonstrate in a very real way what the application will look and feel like, and can also indicate the feasibility of technical components of the system. An advantage of a prototype is that some or all of the programming code in the prototype may be usable in the finished application.

Along with the design documents, another product of system design is the design review sign-off. This is an agreement made by the user organization that the application, if built to the specification, will meet its needs.

A tool that can help to focus your design activities is a matrix of requirements versus system components. This document will also reassure the users that you have accounted for all of the requirements and have a concrete plan for meeting them.

Reminder

If you have reached this point in the development process, you are, by definition, working on a fairly large project. Of course, you should always think through what needs to be done before you start doing it, but with smaller scale solutions, correcting errors (or even rebuilding the application), is relatively easy and inexpensive to do. So, there is less at risk by not going through exhaustive system design—that's the nature of desktop development. But in larger applications, with a sizable investment in development time (and possibly hardware and other costs) at stake, it is in everyone's best interests to go through a more rigorous process of defining and documenting exactly what will be built and how all the pieces will fit together.

In addition, this "engineering" approach extends into the testing phase. In design, the users agree that the system, if built to the design specifications, will meet their needs. So the question to be answered in testing is not, "Does the system meet the users' needs?" but rather, "Does the system meet the specifications, which have been certified as meeting the users' needs?" The distinction is important, because bringing user requirements directly into testing (rather than in addition to the specifications) implies that there may be requirements that are not covered in the specifications, which defeats the purpose of the "engineering" approach and may result in scope creep.

Documenting the Design

Diagrams

One or more of the following types of diagrams are usually used on larger development projects, but their use should be encouraged in any situation where they may be helpful for capturing, validating, and communicating various aspects of the business operation under analysis. Keep in mind that each type of diagram illustrates generally one or two aspects of a system; no single diagram can completely describe a system.

Data Flow Diagram

A data flow diagram (DFD) shows the *logical* process and data flows that make up a business function. Strictly speaking, a DFD is not a computer application design tool; it is a business analysis tool. It shows *what* has to be done to transform information coming in into information going *out* of the business function. It does not show physically how the information is processed, stored, or transported, or when actions take place. (In a correct DFD, you would never see the name of a program, but you may see a process object with a three- or four-word logical description of what the program does.) The objects on a DFD are external entities, data flows, data stores, and processes. The DFD helps you understand *what* needs to be done. Once you do, you can begin making decisions about *how* it should be done (e.g., pencil and calculator or Excel).

Entity Relationship Diagram

An entity relationship diagram (ERD) is also a logical view of a business function, but describes the "things" in the real world with which the business function deals. For example, the business function "Manage Human Resources" deals with *employee*, *department*, *dependent*, etc. These are the entities. Relationships also occur in the real world: "An employee belongs to one and only one department;" "A department has zero to any number of employees;" etc. Also illustrated on an ERD are attributes of the entities. Again, these are "real-world" characteristics: An employee has a birthdate, department number, address, some dependents, etc. As you can see, none of this (necessarily) has anything to do with a computer system. The employee information could be stored on an index card or in an SQL Server database. The ERD helps you understand *what* information you need to manage. Once you do, you can begin making decisions about *how* to manage it (e.g., index cards or SQL Server).

Structure Chart

A structure chart looks like an organization chart and shows the hierarchy of physical acts required to perform some function (it is similar to a work breakdown structure in formal project management). At the top of the chart (the "President") is the overall task to be performed, for example, "Update Customer Record." The next level shows the next level of actions necessary to perform this task, for example, "Get Transaction Record," "Get Customer Record from Database," "Back Up Existing Customer Record," etc. The next level would further decompose those steps.

People will frequently use a spreadsheet program to manage all of their information, but in many cases the information would be better managed as a relational database. Using a database management system (DBMS) may seem at first to be more difficult, but when the information you're dealing with reaches a certain level of complexity, forcing it into a spreadsheet can be a losing battle. One reason a database seems "harder" is that there is another level of abstraction: Rather than putting all the data right there in front of you in a single table the way a spreadsheet does, the relational database uses a mysterious art called "normalization" to break the data into multiple tables, which then must be viewed through "queries" or reports. And when a database is structured (or normalized) properly, you'll need to link tables together to get any useful information. But once it is set up, assuming the information to be managed warrants it, a database is much more powerful, yet more flexible and efficient than a spreadsheet.

In broad terms, a database consists of a series of tables, each representing a "real-world" object that the business deals with. Each row in a table represents a specific instance of the object, and the columns contain specific characteristics of that instance. For example, an employee file would have a row for each employee, and a column for each characteristic, such as ID number, First Name, Last Name, Address, etc. Tables are linked to each other through matching values in corresponding fields.

Naming Conventions

In general, each table and field name should meaningfully describe the object and should distinguish it from similarly named objects.

Relational Database: What's the Big Deal?

A common business situation illustrates some advantages of the relational database: Let's say you want to track employees (in a very small company). You might open up Excel, put in some column headings and start entering data, one employee per row. You enter name (first and last in separate columns, right?) address (city, state and zip in separate columns, too) and so on.

You're doing fine until you get to dependents. Some employees have none, most have one or two. You go through all of your index cards and find that the most prolific worker has 5. So you put 5 columns in your spreadsheet, *Dep. 1, Dep. 2*, etc. Most of these cells are blank for most of the employees, and only one employee fills all 5, so there's a lot of wasted space in your file. Also, it probably won't be long before dependent number 6 comes along, forcing you to change your spreadsheet by adding another column, wasting even more space for all the other employees. Plus, all you have is the dependent's name... what about other dependent information you may need to manage?

In a relational database, you would still have your employee table, but it would have no information about dependents. Employees and dependents are two separate (but related) things, so they each get their own table. Your Dependent Table would have at least 4 or 5 columns: The employee's ID number, dependent's first name and last name (don't assume dependents have the same last name as the employee) probably date of birth, and maybe even full address (don't assume all dependents live with the employee).

As for the relationships between our "entities," How many dependents could an employee possibly have? Well, any number from zero on up. With a relational database, it doesn't matter. Each dependent gets his or her own record, no matter how many there are. The DBMS links the two tables by employee number: "Look at an employee record. Take that employee ID over to the Dependent Table and bring me all the records with the same employee ID." Now you have access to the employee, all dependents, and all of the information about all of them.

In database lingo, you have a one-to-many relationship between the Employee Table and the Dependent Table and the employee ID in the Dependent Table is a foreign key.

Look at all of the additional dependent information you can manage in a database. If you'd added those additional columns (times 5 dependents) to your spreadsheet, it would be getting pretty large. And how about a new requirement: to track the employee's work history? No problem... just add another table to the database. So a relational database is really a more realistic "model" of the real world isn't it? That's the essence of Data Modeling and database design: Identify the *things* in the real world that you care about, identify the *relationships* among them, and then identify the *characteristics* of them. That's your database.

▶ Prototyping

Technical Feasibility Prototype

It may be appropriate to build a prototype of some system components to test the technical feasibility of transactions or algorithms, or to evaluate alternatives for other technical aspects of the system. Some or all of the prototype components may be usable in the actual application.

User Interface and Transaction Flow Prototype

A prototype of the screens and transaction flow is an excellent way to demonstrate the look and feel of an application for the users.

▶ Scope Freeze

Scope freeze is the point in the development process when no more changes can be accepted without jeopardizing the delivery of the finished system. Actual implementation of scope freeze and its placement in the lifecycle depend in large part on the development tool and methodology being used. For example, in a prototyping development process (build, expand, and refine), scope freeze may not be necessary; with a sound data infrastructure and flexible user-interface tool, the essence of development is constant improvement through the incremental addition of new features. However, in a larger project where, for example, coordination of different organizations or multiple developers is necessary, failure to draw the line on major changes while the system is still in development may mean that it never gets out the door.

To prevent scope creep, identify and document the system requirements carefully and thoroughly, design your solution to meet all of those requirements, then work with the users to balance the technical and business needs to plan a release schedule, with the most important features in the first release and other enhancements later. Also, make sure the users understand scope freeze.

▶ Testing (End-User Acceptance)

As the development phase progresses, you'll want to start planning for testing. Testing is essentially a verification process: Based on the system specifications, you know what to expect from the system in operation, so the essential question in testing is: "Do you see what was expected; does the system meet the specifications?" If so, breathe a sigh of relief. If not, why? Is it a bug in the code? Was the definition of a requirement incomplete or ambiguous? Note that the essential question of testing is not, "Does the system meet the users' requirements?" That question at this point in the process implies that there may be requirements that were not covered by the specifications.

The key players in the project should be very familiar with the design specifications and how they, point-for-point, address the user requirements. Creating test plans and test cases is a refinement of those points in a very tangible, detailed way. Test plans should cover both user functionality and technical operation of the system.

The result of the testing process is user acceptance that the system works as specified.

Test Plans and Cases

See Table C–1 for an example of a user test plan and Table C–2 for an example of a technical test plan.

Table C–1 User Test Plan Example

Plan 1: Verify that customer account maintenance works correctly (Requirement #12)

Case	Task	Conditions	Expected Results	Bug Notes and Report Number
Case 1: Add account to database *Requirement 12.1*	Execute "Add Customer" transaction	User ID: Jerry X Customer Name: Buck Clayton Address: … Phone: …	Operator receives message #1320 "Customer Record Added." Tomorrow's Customer Activity Report (report A-22) includes the new customer. Report shows customer information as entered in the "Add Customer" transaction. Report shows correct system-generated account number, operator ID, and date/time stamp. Weekly Operator Performance Review report (report B-60) for Jerry X includes the "Add Customer" transaction with the correct date and time.	Transaction appears on B-60, but operator name and date/time are missing. BUG #68
Case 2: Enter duplicate customer record *Requirement 12.2*	Execute "Add Customer" transaction	Same as above	Operator receives message #126, "Customer Record Already Exists." Generate e-mail message #12 to supervisor: "Investigate Duplicate Customer Record." Tomorrow's Customer Activity Report (report A-22) shows the attempted duplicate entry with operator ID and date/time stamp. Weekly Operator Performance Review report (report B-60) for Jerry shows the attempted duplicate entry with correct date/time stamp.	Operator received message #113, "Record Deleted" BUG #69

147

Table C–1 User Test Plan Example *continued*

Plan 1: Verify that customer account maintenance works correctly (Requirement #12)

Case	Task	Conditions	Expected Results	Bug Notes and Report Number
Case 2: Update customer record *Requirement 12.3*	Execute "Update Customer" transaction	Same as above, except new address: xxxx	Operator receives message #144, "Record Updated."	(OK)
Case 4: Delete customer record *Requirement 12.4*	Execute "Delete Customer" transaction	Same as above	Operator receives message #113, "Record Deleted." Tomorrow's Customer Activity Report (report A-22) shows the deletion with operator ID and date/time stamp. Weekly Operator Performance Review report (report B-60) for Jerry X shows the delete transaction with correct date/time stamp.	(OK)

Table C–2 Technical Test Plan Example

Plan 1: Verify Concurrent Record Access handling (Record Locking)

Case	Task	Conditions *Note: Always record date and time of transaction*	Expected Results	Bug Notes and Report Number
Case 1: Delete record being edited by another user *Requirement 18.1*	User A: Execute "Update Customer Record" transaction. User B: Execute "Delete Customer Record" while record is open for editing	Both transactions access account # 33234, customer Al Grey	User A receives message # 161; User B # 161; User B	
Case 2: Delete record being browsed by another user *Requirement 18.2*	User A: Execute "View Customer Record" transaction. User B: Execute "Delete Customer Record" transaction while record is open for viewing	Both transactions access account # 33238, customer Jo Jones	User A receives message # 171; User B receives message #178.	

149

Executing the Test Plan

To begin testing, you'll need to load initial data into the system's tables from existing files or external sources (be sure to allow time for debugging any conversion programs and verifying that the data was loaded properly). Next, submit the transactions as specified in the test plans. Reviewing all test results is important, but it is particularly crucial for transactions that set up later test transactions. For example, a transaction to delete an account must be preceded by the transaction that adds the account in the first place. Undetected failure of the add transaction could cause a delay in completing the test of the delete transaction.

Rework

When creating your project plan, be realistic about allowing time to fix problems and retesting. Assuming that the system will be built perfectly bug-free will surely cause you to miss your delivery deadline.

Acceptance

At the completion of testing, the user manager should provide a written certification that the system performs the way everyone agreed it would.

Pilot Test

A pilot test is required for all new applications to validate the deployment strategy and identify issues that may arise in production. Schedule the pilot test far enough in advance of the implementation date so that any issues can be resolved. The pilot test takes place in a preproduction, live environment with a subset of users.

IT Pilot

An IT pilot run can be used to identify and resolve infrastructure issues.

Parallel Test

If the new application is a replacement for an existing manual or automated process, a parallel test is recommended. Process the same transactions through both systems and verify that the results are as expected.

Training

Training and documentation requirements are generally determined by the nature of the application (number of reports, transactions, etc.) and the number of system users. Be sure to review your user requirements with the training manager to determine the best approach to training and documentation. Training is also an important element in marketing an application. Scheduling and publicizing training courses can help to increase interest in the application and its utilization, as well as make the users more proficient.

Course and Documentation Development

For as few as 8 to 10 users, the Desktop Training Group will develop and deliver a training course for an application. For documentation, if the number of users is small (up to a dozen or so), a quick reference guide may be all that is necessary. For a larger number of users or a complex application, you may need to plan for a more complete user guide.

Timing

To develop training and documentation, the Training Group needs to get involved in the project when it is complete enough to be demonstrated.

Resources

For a training course, the users will need to provide business rules and/or a case study. Also, if the application involves a database, you will need to provide a nonproduction database for use in training sessions.

System Administration Tasks

Most desktop applications are designed with intuitive navigation (following Windows® conventions) and are so tailored to the users' operations that only minimal training may be necessary in many cases. However, training and documentation may be required for system administration, such as:

- Managing external data feeds (downloading files, loading floppies or CDs, converting data, etc.)
- Managing data backups and restorations

Identify any such requirements and include them in your project plan.

▶ Support

Be sure to include in your project plan a notification to the help desk about your application and its scheduled implementation date. Also be sure to provide them with any necessary training and documentation for supporting the users.

▶ Marketing

The project champion works with the Training Group to publicize a new application through e-mail announcements and training classes. These are effective methods of increasing awareness and use of the application. To maximize effectiveness, they must be scheduled carefully to coincide with the rollout of the application. The project champion may also publicize the application within the business unit with e-mail announcements, etc.

▶ Implementation

Technical Standards

Implementation varies by tool: SMS or WINBATCH with .INI file.

All desktop development should be designed for a specific screen resolution (e.g., 800 x 600) and a standard color scheme. All user workstations should be set to these properties.

Rollout Plan

Your project plan should include detailed steps to roll out the application, including any data conversion, desktop deployment, etc., activities that may be required.

▶ Maintenance/Change Control

Once a system is in production, it may be necessary to make changes. Changes may be initiated by a technology organization (moving the application to a different server, for example) or by the users to fix bugs or enhance functionality. A System Change Request Form (see Figure C–1) should always be completed to document changes and assess their effect on business operations and technical resources.

▶ Postimplementation Follow-Up

After a new application has been operating for a while, it's time to step back and see if it is producing the results expected. This is an often overlooked phase, but it is really one of the most important, since it's the method by which we measure how closely we hit the mark with the project. It helps the business users judge whether they are getting the results they expected and thus whether a particular allocation of company resources was effective. Also, it helps IT in improving the development process.

It is a good idea to think about this phase at the beginning of your project; if you intend to measure changes in business unit performance, customer satisfaction, etc., after a new process is implemented, you'll need baseline measures from before it is implemented.

System Performance

Operational Measures

Production-type work is usually the easiest to measure, so it's the work that gets measured most. It's easiest to see the effects of a new process or application. For example, let's say the month before a new system

DESKTOP DEVELOPMENT	SYSTEM CHANGE REQUEST	Requester Name		Requester Phone

Requester Name | **Requester Phone**

Date of Request | **Date Change is Required** | **Application Platform**
☐ Access   ☐ Outlook/Exchange   ☐ Excel

Application System/Subsystem | **Desktop Development Analyst**

Please describe the change.

Please describe what is required to make the change and put it into effect.

Instructions
1. Please complete all information above to request a system change.
2. All changes are thoroughly tested in the QA environment prior to moving.
3. Please plan changes far in advance to allow time for development and testing.

Figure C-1 System Change Request Form

installation, the user group processed 100 transactions per hour; 4 months after the new system was installed (allowing time for everyone to learn and get comfortable with the new methods), the user group processed 150 transactions per hour. Was that the productivity gain expected? Is it larger or smaller than expected? Why? If smaller, is there anything to do to improve it? If larger, could other groups benefit similarly?

Doing a cost/benefit analysis early in the lifecycle gives you a great advantage in doing these kinds of evaluations. The users should certainly know going into a project what it is they want to accomplish and how the results will affect their bottom line: Does that 50 additional transactions mean 50% more revenue? Does it mean the manager can reassign some of the staff to other responsibilities? And from a financial point of view, what is the return on investment of the new system? How long will it take for the increased revenue or avoided costs to pay back the cost of creating the new system?

Operational measures extend to customers too, particularly with systems that support them directly (common now with Web applications) or that support customer representatives (e.g., call center or order fulfillment applications). Customer surveys before and after implementation of any new process can demonstrate improved service and customer satisfaction.

User Satisfaction

There is a lot to be learned by measuring how users feel about a system. They are usually the best source for ideas on improving the user interface or any bottlenecks in system performance, for example. A carefully designed user survey is a good way to obtain this feedback, and is preferable to user-initiated anecdotal "evidence." The former will generally give you a clear indication of any shortcomings, allow you to evaluate them in proper perspective, and thus set overall priorities for improvement; the latter may tend to emphasize the most negative aspects and lack perspective. Another source of information is records from the help desk. If patterns appear in the questions coming in from the users, it may indicate that, for example, some sort of educational remedy may be called for (e.g., a reference card, additional training, or even an e-mail to the users on how to avoid common problems).

Technical Measures

Any available technical measures, such as transaction volumes, table growth, etc., should be reviewed periodically to avoid problems such as running out of disk space. Plus, user satisfaction depends a great deal on system performance. As a system becomes more heavily used, you may need to consider moving it to a dedicated server, beefing up communication lines, etc.

Process Performance

Analysts and developers should take some time to look back at projects from the IT perspective, to judge how well the development process worked. Some questions to ask: Were the requirements gathering complete or did parts of the system have to be redesigned? Were any players caught unaware of their responsibilities due to communication failures? Were resource requirements and timelines accurately estimated? Did everyone learn more about how the business works so a better analysis job can be done next time?

Systems Development Contract

▶ User Responsibilities

Project Ownership

The user project champion should have the successful project delivery on his or her PMP.

Dedicated Resources

1. User project manager (project champion)
   a) A user project manager will be assigned whose role will be to represent all users. He or she will ensure that the user community speaks with one voice when defining the business requirements.
   b) The user project manager should be a dedicated resource whose top priority is ensuring that user-related tasks are completed. These tasks include the following: requirements gathering, system design, user testing, and user training.
   c) The user project manager has the authority to make design decisions and prioritize deliverables.

2. User test team
   a) This should consist of users who can test the application and give worthwhile feedback.
   b) These users need to be dedicated resources.

Sign-Off

Users will provide written sign-off on critical project documentation.

System Change Control

The process by which system changes are requested and approved will be formalized. Senior management must approve significant changes that affect the project plan.

Prioritization of Deliverables

Users will prioritize the project deliverables into manageable pieces to limit the risk associated with complex projects.

Time Management

1. All meetings should have an agenda and should include the personnel necessary to make decisions. Business-related decisions should not be made in prototype review sessions and/or project status meetings.
2. Project-related tasks should be scheduled in advance. The project schedule should include vacations and other commitments.

▶ IT Responsibilities

Project Ownership

The IT project champion should have the successful project delivery on his or her PMP.

Estimates

IT will provide high-level estimates for major project deliverables during the project initiation phase. As the requirements are analyzed, these estimates will be adjusted and detailed in a full project plan.

Project Documentation

IT will provide clear and concise business requirement documents, free of technical jargon and technical-related issues, to facilitate user sign-off.

Project Delays

1. IT will report project delays in a timely manner so the user community can adjust their business plans accordingly.
2. IT will explain the cause of the delay: for example, a change in requirements, an underestimate, or a reprioritization.

Application Prototypes

IT will provide application prototypes during the analysis phase to facilitate requirements gathering and finalizing the functional specifications.

A prototype should describe the application's look and feel, the contents of the database, and how the application will be used. It should NOT enforce business rules, perform database updates, or reflect actual system performance.

System Testing

IT should thoroughly test all software prior to initiating the user test phase. Basic errors, such as the inability to save data, should be debugged during system testing.

Time Management

1. All meetings should have an agenda and should include the personnel necessary to make decisions. Technical decisions should not be made in prototype review sessions and/or project status meetings.
2. Project-related tasks should be scheduled in advance. The project schedule should include vacations and other commitments.

Index

A

Accurate skills assessments, 70
Actions, investing in, 6
Admitting mistakes, 93
Alignment:
    with the business, 4, 55–56
    evolution of, 59
    technology, 56–58
Analyst workstation, and value
    communication, 34–36
Anytime/anywhere courses, 69
Application Architecture Group, 56
Application prototypes, and IT project
    champion, 159
Application requirements, 136–37
    diagrams, 136
    narrative, 136
    similar applications, 137
Application spectrum, 32–33
    and the Desktop Development Group,
      63–64
Application suitability, for Desktop
    Development Group, 65
Applications Architecture Group, 57–58,
    130–32
    architecture function, 58
    charter, 130
    forms of engagement, 130–31
    involvement of, 132
    mission, 130
    roles of, 131
Applications development staff, and
    matrix organizations, 55–56
Authority, delegation of, 91

B

Big-picture thinking, 16–18
Boehringer Ingelheim, 42–44
    corporate vision, foundation of, 43
    Value Through Innovation, 42
    vision statement, 42
Brevity, in communication, 94
Business cases, 26, 32, 46
Business continuity, and disaster recovery,
    41
Business objectives, alignment with, for
    jointly developed business cases, 26
Business rule management, and the
    Desktop Development Group, 62
Business strategy formation process,
    40–42
Business teams, 4, 27

C

Candidate profile, 79
Candor, 89
Career path, 76
CEO:
    education, 100–101
    flying solo, 102
    leadership, 99–100
    leadership, partnership, education
     (LPE) model, 102
    partnership, 100
    roles/responsibilities of, 99–102
Charter, 138
    Applications Architecture Group, 130
    Desktop Development Group, 117–18
    Help desk, 122
    project acceptance, 138
    second-level support, 129
    technical support, 128–29
    training department, 118–19
Clarity, in communication, 94
Comments, personalizing, 94
Common language, 18–22
Communication, 18–22, 76
    brevity in, 94
    clarity in, 94
    over-communication, 28
    of project acceptance, 138

of the small picture, 49–50
    value, 34–37
    and analyst workstation, 34–36
    and IT business partners, 34
    and workflow manager, 36–37
Consequence-based thinking, 9–23, 11
    and creativity, 10
    and decisions/actions, 10
    defined, 10–11
    hallmarks of environment, 9–10
    right/wrong trap,\rdblquote 12–13
    situation, decision, and consequence
     model, 11
Consequence-minded decisions, 12
    and workgroups, 14
Consulting management, and the Desktop
    Development Group, 62
Contact information, 23
Corporate citizenship, 94
Cost/benefit analysis/feasibility study,
    137–38
    IT resources/costs, 137
    user priorities, 137
Cost center, transition to a business
    partner, 76
Course and documentation development,
    70
Creativity, and consequence-based
    thinking, 10
Credit-taking, 95
Customer Relationship Management
    (CRM), 3

D

Data center organization, 58
Data consistency, and the Desktop
    Development Group, 62
Data flow diagram (DFD), 142
Decentralized decision-making, 91
Decision-making, 89
    and consequence-based thinking, 10

decentralized, 91
Dedicated resources, and user project champion, 158–59
Deficiencies, highlighting, 94
Delegation of authority, 91
Delegation of responsibility and authority to lowest possible level, 76, 77
Deliverables, prioritization of, 159
Design, 140–45
data flow diagram (DFD), 142
diagrams, 142
documenting, 142
    entity relationship diagram (ERD), 142–43
    guidelines/standards/procedures, 66–67
    naming conventions, 144
    relational database guidelines, 144–45
    structure chart, 143
Desktop Development Group, 60, 62–68, 82, 117–18
and the application spectrum, 63–64
application suitability for, 65
benefits of, 118
business rule management, 62
charter, 117–18
consulting management, 62
data consistency, 62
design, 140–45
data flow diagram (DFD), 142
diagrams, 142
documenting, 142
    entity relationship diagram (ERD), 142–43
    naming conventions, 144
    relational database guidelines, 144–45
    structure chart, 143
design guidelines/standards/procedures, 66–67
desktop development services, 62
expanded uses of data, 62
formalizing/documenting the standards and practices of, 63
implementation, 152–53
rollout plan, 153
technical standards, 152
maintenance/change control, 153
marketing, 152
mission, 117
naming conventions, 67
post-implementation follow-up, 153–56
standards and procedures, 72–73
project acceptance, 138–39
approval/communication, 138
charter, 138
project lifecycle, 133–34
high-level requirements, gathering, 134
notifications, 134
request management, 133–34
project planning, 139–40
activities, 140
prototyping, 145
quick start guide, 65
relational database guidelines, 67–68
requirements gathering/analysis, 135–38
application requirements, 136–37
cost/benefit analysis/feasibility study, 137–38
results, 135
role definition/notification, 136
scope freeze, 145–46

staff utilization, 62–63
standards/procedures, 133–56
support, 152
testing (end-user acceptance), 146–52
acceptance, 150
executing the test plan, 150
pilot test, 150–51
rework, 150
test plans and cases, 146
training, 151–52
third-level support and management, 62
tool utilization, 63
top nine list, 65
Desktop development services, 57
the Desktop Development Group, 62
Diagrams, 142
Disaster recovery, and business continuity, 41
Documentation requirements, 70
Documentation, training department, 68–69
Documenting standards/practices, and the Desktop Development Group, 63

E

End-user acceptance:
acceptance, 150
executing the test plan, 150
pilot test, 150–51
IT pilot, 150–51
parallel test, 150–51
rework, 150
test plans and cases, 146
training, 151–52
Enterprise acquisition strategy, 40
Enterprise objective, 89–90
Enterprise Resource Planning (ERP) systems, 3
Enterprise strategy, 41–42
Enterprise vision, 42–44, 100
Entity relationship diagram (ERD), 142–43
Estimates, and IT project champion, 158
Evolution of alignment, 59
Evolution, training department, 68–73
Expanded uses of data, and the Desktop Development Group, 62
Experience, compromising on, 79

F

Fairrals, Mitch, contact information, 23
Formalizing standards/practices, and the Desktop Development Group, 63
Function-based training, 69

G

Geek speak, translating, 50–52
Global Application Development Group, 58
Global business unit view, global organization matrix, 25
Global organization matrix, 25–26

H

Help desk, 57, 122
charter, 122
mission, 122
sample Help Desk customer service survey, 123–28
Hershey Foods Corporation, 44
High-level requirements, gathering, 134
Hiring, 77–79
Honesty/candor, 90

Human capital management, 75–83
compensation package, 77–78
interviewers, training of, 78
interviews, 78–79
managing the process, 80–81
mentoring, 80
organization as a career, 82–83
performance management process (PMP), 81–82
quality of life, 76, 77
recruiting/hiring, 77–79
subordinate interviews, 79
transition planning, 80
Human Resources (HR) Department, 79

I

Ideal IT environment, signs of, 75
Implementation, 71, 152–53
rollout plan, 153
technical standards, 152
In-house systems, online help files for, 69
Information overload, 93–94
Information technology, (See IT)
Integrity, 90
Interviews, 78–79
candidate profile, 79
experience, compromising on, 79
subordinate, 79
Investing:
in actions, 6
in values, 6–7
IT:
evolution of, 3, 28
as an investment, 5
managing as a cost center vs. managing as an investment, 29
managing as a strategic asset, 4
marketing of, 30
partnering within, 28–30
pilot, 150–51

L

Leadership, partnership, education (LPE) model, 102
Legacy applications, 95
Living above the line, 15, 18
Living below the line, 15, 18
Local view, global organization matrix, 25

M

Maintenance/change control, 153
Managing the process, 80–81
Marketing, 71, 152
Matrix organizations:
and applications development staff, 55–56
business priority, 56
defined, 55
management principles, 56
shared services, 56
systems manager, 56
Meeting management, 52–53
Mentoring, 57, 80, 92
Mission statement, 18, 89
Saturn Car Company values, 97
Mistakes, admitting, 93

N

Naming conventions, 67, 144
New employees, training plans for, 70
Notifications, 134

O

On The Mark, 23

Online help files for in-house systems, 69
Organization, 55–73
    alignment, evolution of, 59
    alignment with the business, 55–56
    as a career, 82–83
    technology alignment, 56–58
    training department evolution, 68–73
Over-communication, 28

P

Parallel test, 150–51
Partnering, 4, 25–30, 92–93
    business cases, 26
    business teams, 27
    within IT, 28–30
    with senior management, 100
Perfection, avoiding demands of, 93
Performance management process (PMP),
    81–82
    importance of, 46–47
    key points of, 82
Performance, recognizing, 95
Personal Productivity Services Group, 56,
    57, 82–83
    desktop data explosion, 61
    and Desktop Development Group, 60,
    62
    desktop tools, 61–62
    information management, 60–61
    organizations of, 60
    training function, 60
Personal productivity services
    organization:
    Applications Architecture Group,
    130–32
    Desktop Development Group, 117–18
    Help desk, 122
        sample Help Desk customer
        service survey, 123–28
    overview, 117–32
    second-level support, 129
    technical support, 128–29
    training department, 118–22
Personalizing comments, avoidance of, 94
Pilot test, 150–51
    IT pilot, 150–51
    parallel test, 150–51
Planning:
    meetings, 53
    project, 139–40
    transition, 80
Post-implementation follow-up, 153–56
process performance, 73, 156
    standards and procedures, 72–73
    system performance, 72
    operational measures, 153–55
    technical measures, 73, 156
    user satisfaction, 72–73, 155
Preparedness, 90
Presentation, training courses in, 53
Prioritization of deliverables, and user
    project champion, 159
Process performance, 73
Professionalism, 90
Progress, measuring, 47
Project acceptance, 138–39
    approval/communication, 138
    charter, 138
Project delays, and IT project champion,
    159
Project document, and IT project
    champion, 159
Project leaders, 80
Project lifecycle, 133–34
    high-level requirements, gathering,
    134

notifications, 134
    request management, 133–34
Project ownership:
    and IT project champion, 158
    and user project champion, 158
Project planning, 139–40
    activities, 140
Prototyping, 145

Q

Quality of life, 76, 77
    and values, 85
Quick start guide, Desktop Development
    Group, 65

R

Realistic course evaluations, 70
Reaping the hidden harvest, 95–96
Recognizing performance, 95
Recruiting/hiring, 77–79
Regional view, global organization
    matrix, 25
Relational database guidelines, 67–68,
    144–45
Relationships:
    delegating upwards, 5
    emphasis on, 92–93
    importance of, 4–5
Request management, 133–34
Requirements gathering/analysis, 135–38
    application requirements, 136–37
    diagrams, 136
    narrative, 136
    similar applications, 137
    cost/benefit analysis/feasibility study,
    137–38
    IT resources/costs, 137
    user priorities, 137, 135
role definition/notification, 136
    "Right/wrong trap" 12–13
Rollout plan, 71, 153

S

Sample business case template, 103–16
    document, 103–4
    amendment history, 104
    purpose, 104
    estimated annual operation cost, 107
    estimated start-up costs, 107
    financial summary, 105
    preliminary requirements, 106–7
    project scope, 106
    time/cost estimates, 106–7
    project summary, 104–5
    action steps, 105
    overview, 104
    strategic rationale, 104
    project team, 105–6
    extended team, 106
    management team, 105–6
    risks, 108
    sign-off, 109
    supporting information, 105–6
Saturn Car Company, 96–97
Saturn Car Company values:
    mission statement, 97
    values, 97
Scope creep, 93
Scope freeze, 145–46
Second-level support, 129
    benefits, 129
    charter, 129
    mission, 129
Senior management, partnership with, 100
Sharing the spotlight, 95

Sign-off, and user project champion, 159
Situation, decision, and consequence
    model, 11
Situation-minded decisions, 12
    communicating, 49–50
    geek speak, translating, 50–52
    meeting management, 52–53
Solution seeking, 94
Staff, investing in, 76
Staff turnover, 76
Staff utilization, and the Desktop
    Development Group, 62–63
Standards, 57
Strategic thinking, 39–40
Strategy, 39–47
    and adequate objectives, 45
    business cases, 46
    business strategy formation process,
    41–42
    enterprise vision, 42–44
    making operational, 46
    performance management process,
    importance of, 46–47
    progress, measuring, 47
    technology strategy creation, 45
    technology vision, 44
Structure chart, 143
Successful communication, defined, 22
Successful technology strategy,
    characteristics of, 45
Supply Chain Management (SCM)
    systems, 3
Support, 71, 152
Support services, 57
SWAT team resources, 57
System administrative tasks, 71
System change control, and user project
    champion, 159
System change request form, 154
System performance, 72
System testing, and IT project champion,
    159
Systems development contract, 157–59
    IT responsibilities, 158–59
        application prototypes, 159
        estimates, 158
        project delays, 159
        project ownership, 158
        projet document, 159
        system testing, 159
        time management, 159
    user responsibilities, 157–58
        dedicated resources, 158–59
        prioritization of deliverables, 159
        project ownership, 158
        sign-off, 159
        system change control, 159
        time management, 159

T

Tapping in, 18–20
    defined, 18
Technical feasibility prototype, 145
Technical solutions, 57–58
Technical standards, 152
Technical support, 128–29
    charter, 128–29
    mission, 128
    second-level support, 129
Technical Support Group, 60
Technical test plan example, 149
Technology alignment, 56–58
    Applications Architecture Group, 57–58
    Personal Productivity Services Group,
    57
Technology strategy creation, 45

Technology vision, 44
Testing (end-user acceptance), 146–52
    acceptance, 150
    executing the test plan, 150
    pilot test, 150–51
        IT pilot, 150–51
        parallel test, 150–51
        rework, 150
        test plans and cases, 146
        training, 151–52
    course and documentation
        development, 151
    resources, 151
    system administration tasks, 152
    timing, 151
Third-level support and management, and
        the Desktop Development Group,
        62
Thoroughness, 90
Time management:
    and IT project champion, 159
    and user project champion, 159
Tool utilization, and the Desktop
        Development Group, 63
Top nine list, Desktop Development
        Group, 65
Training, 57, 76
    course and documentation
        development, 151
    of interviewers, 78
    in presentation/written
        communication, 53
    resources, 151
    system administration tasks, 152
    timing, 151
Training department, 118–22
    accurate skills assessments, 70
    anytime/anywhere courses, 69
    benefits of, 119–22
    charter, 118–19
    communications/marketing, 120,
        121–22
    course and documentation
        development, 70
    documentation, 68–69, 119–20
    documentation development, 119,
        121
    evolution, 68–73

function-based training, 69
implementation, 71
marketing, 71
miscellaneous tasks, 121
mission, 118
online help files for in-house systems,
    69
post-implementation follow-up
    standards/procedures, 72–73
presentation support, 121
realistic course evaluations, 70
representation of IT, 118–19
resources, 70
rollout plan, 71
rollouts, 121
statistics, 121
support, 71
system administrative tasks, 71
timing, 70
training administration, 118–19
training and documentation require-
    ments, 70
training delivery, 120–21, 122
training development, 119, 121
training plans for new employees, 70
training standards/procedures, 70–71
Training Group, 82–83
Training standards/procedures, 70–71
Transition planning, 80

U

User interface and transaction flow
    prototype, 145
User satisfaction, 72–73, 155
User test plan example, 147–48

V

Value chain, 1–3
Value communication, 34–37
    and analyst workstation, 34–36
    and IT business partners, 34
    and workflow manager, 36–37
Value management, 29–37
Value, recognizing, 30
Values:
    actions as a result of, 91–95
    admitting mistakes, 93

avoiding perfection, 93
corporate citizenship, 94
decentralized decision-making, 91
delegation of authority, 91
emphasis on relationships, 92–93
information overload, 93–94
legacy applications, 95
mentoring, 92
personalizing comments, avoidance
    of, 94
recognizing performance, 95
sharing the spotlight, 95
solution seeking, 94
    anticipation of all questions, 90
    contract formed by, 85
    defined, 7, 85
    enterprise objective, 89–90
    giving their D.U.E., 86
    honesty/candor, 90
    integrity, 90
    investing in, 6–7, 85–97
    loyalty, 86
    mutual respect, 87–88
    no surprises, 87
    preparedness, 90
    and principled actions, 85
    professionalism, 90
    and quality of life, 85
    reaping the hidden harvest, 95–96
    Saturn Car Company, 96–97
    team responsibility taking, 88
    thoroughness, 90
Vision, 4, 18
    enterprise, 42–44
    technology, 44
Vision statements, fundamental principles
    of, 42

W

Workflow manager, and value
    communication, 36–37
Workgroups, and consequence-minded
    decisions, 14
Workstation, analyst, and value
    communication, 34–36
Written communication, training courses
    in, 53